THIMBLEBERRIES®

Block by Block
to Beautiful Quilts

BY LYNETTE JENSEN

Landauer Publishing

THIMBLEBERRIES®

Block by Block
to Beautiful Quilts

Copyright© 2009 by Landauer Corporation

Projects Copyright© 2009 by Lynette Jensen

This book was designed, produced, and published by Landauer Publishing
A division of Landauer Corporation
3100 NW 101st Street, Urbandale, Iowa 50322
www.landauercorp.com 800/557-2144

President: Jeramy Lanigan Landauer
Vice President of Sales & Operations: Kitty Jacobson
Managing Editor: Jeri Simon
Art Director: Laurel Albright
Photographer: Craig Anderson Studios, Sue Voegtlin

For Thimbleberries®:
Creative Director: Lynette Jensen
Technical Writer: Sue Bahr
Technical Illustrator: Lisa Kirchoff

We also wish to thank the support staff of the Thimbleberries® Design Studio:
Sherry Husske, Virginia Brodd, Renae Ashwill, Ardelle Paulson, Julie Jergens,
Clarine Howe, Tracy Schrantz, Amy Albrecht, Leone Rusch, and Connie Albin.

The following manufacturers are licensed to sell Thimbleberries® products:
Thimbleberries® Rugs (www.colonialmills.com); Thimbleberries® Quilt
Stencils (www.quiltingcreations.com); and Thimbleberries® Fabrics (RJR Fabrics
available at independent quilt shops).

This book is printed on acid-free paper.

Printed in China 10 9 8 7 6 5 4 3 2 1

Library of Congress Control Number: 2009927748

ISBN 13: 978-0-9818040-6-4
ISBN 10: 0-9818040-6-3

Foreword

Years ago, I created Thimbleberries®
Block-of-the-Month program as a way to
enable quilters with limited time to create
quilts of enduring beauty. Quilters worldwide embraced the concept. Today,
Thimbleberries Block-of-the-Month programs are a staple in the quilting
industry. Thousands of quilters take part in Thimbleberries® Clubs that meet
monthly in 1000 shops.

In this book, I've assembled some of my most popular traditional pieced block
motifs and present them in a variety of color options and patterns to provide you
with choices for creating a myriad of beautiful quilt projects for your home.

From collection to collection, from season to season and from year to year you
can create with confidence knowing that the Thimbleberries color palette will
always blend beautifully and will stand the test of time.

To help you successfully complete your quilts, my staff and I have worked hard
to create a system of quilt-making that uses clear and simple instructions you
can rely on. Even first-time quilters can build confidence and skills.

Whichever project you choose — a bed quilt, table runner, pillow or wall quilt—
enjoy the journey of creating beautiful quilted keepsakes that welcome family and
friends to a warm and inviting home.

My best,

Lynette Jensen

Vintage Stitches

contents

Vintage Stitches
Quilt
8

Vintage Stitches
Pillow
28

Four Seasons

contents

5

Crazy Quilt Puzzle Quilt

contents

Color Option—Autumn

Color Option—Winter

Hometown Christmas

contents

Vintage Stitches

The blending of color, design, pattern and piecing in the 12-block *Vintage Stitches Quilt* reflects the visual artistry that's the hallmark of Thimbleberries' excellence.

Each block is surprisingly simple, yet beautifully engaging. The floral focus fabric centered in each unique Thimbleberries'-created block is enhanced by traditional pieced geometric shapes. Repeat the floral fabric in the border and frame the blocks with a traditional lattice setting and you have just completed a stunning heirloom quilt to be treasured for generations.

VINTAGE STITCHES QUEEN SIZE QUILT
92 x 110-inches

Fabrics & Supplies

3-5/8 yards **LARGE FLORAL** for all blocks, outer border (cut on lengthwise grain)

2-1/4 yards **BEIGE PRINT #1** for background in all blocks

1/8 yard **PINK PRINT** for block 1

1/8 yard **GREEN PRINT** for block 1

1/4 yard **DARK ROSE PRINT** for block 2

1/8 yard **GREEN PRINT** for block 2

1/4 yard **YELLOW FLORAL** for block 3

1/8 yard **BLUE/GREEN PRINT** for block 3

1/8 yard **GREEN PRINT** for block 4

1/8 yard **BLUE PRINT** for block 4

1/8 yard **LIGHT TEAL PRINT** for block 5

1/8 yard **LIGHT PINK PRINT** for block 5

1/8 yard **PINK PRINT** for block 6

1/8 yard **BLUE FLORAL** for block 6

1/4 yard **DARK GREEN PRINT** for block 7

1/8 yard **LIGHT BLUE PRINT** for block 7

1/4 yard **GOLD PRINT** for block 8

1/4 yard **PINK/YELLOW PRINT** for block 8

1/8 yard **YELLOW PRINT** for block 9

1-1/4 yards **GREEN PRINT** for block 9, flying geese border

1/8 yard **BROWN/GREEN PRINT** for block 10

1/4 yard **ROSE/BROWN PRINT** for block 10

1/8 yard **TONAL ROSE PRINT** for block 11

1/8 yard **GREEN PRINT** for block 11

1/4 yard **LIGHT ROSE PRINT** for block 12

3-1/8 yards **BROWN PRINT** for block 12, block borders, lattice strips, inner border, middle border

1-1/3 yards **BEIGE PRINT #2** for flying geese border

1 yard **GREEN PRINT** for binding

3-1/4 yards for 108-inch wide backing
OR
8-1/4 yards for 44-inch wide backing

quilt batting, at least 98 x 116-inches

Before beginning this project, read through **Getting Started** *on page 145.*

Note: *Each of the 12 pieced blocks has a 6-1/2-inch* **LARGE FLORAL** *center square. You can cut the squares as you make each block or cut them all at once.*

Refer to this cutting to cut the squares all at once:

From **LARGE FLORAL**:
- Cut 2, 6-1/2 x 44-inch strips.
  From strips cut: 12, 6-1/2-inch squares

Vintage Stitches
Block One

Cutting

From LARGE FLORAL:
• Cut 1, 6-1/2-inch square

From PINK PRINT:
• Cut 1, 1-1/2 x 44-inch strip. From strip cut:
  4, 1-1/2 x 6-1/2-inch rectangles

From BEIGE PRINT #1:
• Cut 1, 2-7/8 x 14-inch strip
• Cut 1, 2-1/2 x 44-inch strip. From strip cut:
  4, 2-1/2 x 4-1/2-inch rectangles
  4, 2-1/2-inch squares
  4, 1-1/2-inch squares

From GREEN PRINT:
• Cut 1, 2-7/8 x 14-inch strip
• Cut 1, 2-1/2 x 22-inch strip. From strip cut:
  8, 2-1/2-inch squares

Piecing

Step 1 Sew 1-1/2 x 6-1/2-inch **PINK** rectangles to top/bottom edges of the 6-1/2-inch **LARGE FLORAL** square; press. Sew 1-1/2-inch **BEIGE #1** squares to both ends of remaining 1-1/2 x 6-1/2-inch **PINK** rectangles; press. Sew rectangles to side edges of the **LARGE FLORAL** square; press. <u>At this point the unit should measure 8-1/2-inches square.</u>

Make 1

Step 2 With right sides together, layer 2-7/8 x 14-inch **BEIGE #1** and **GREEN** strips. Press together, but do not sew. Cut layered strip into squares. Cut each layered square in half diagonally to make 8 sets of triangles. Stitch 1/4-inch from diagonal edge of each set of triangles; press.

Crosscut 4, 2-7/8-inch squares

Make 8, 2-1/2-inch triangle-pieced squares

Step 3 With right sides together, position a 2-1/2-inch **GREEN** square on the corner of a 2-1/2 x 4-1/2-inch **BEIGE #1** rectangle. Draw diagonal line on square and stitch on line. Trim seam allowance to 1/4-inch; press. Repeat this process at opposite corner of rectangle. Sew a triangle-pieced square to both ends of each unit; press.

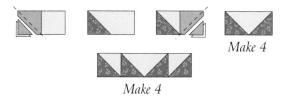

Make 4

Make 4

Step 4 Sew Step 3 units to top/bottom edges of Step 1 center unit; press. Sew 2-1/2-inch **BEIGE #1** squares to both ends of remaining Step 3 units; press. Sew the units to side edges of center unit; press. <u>At this point the block should measure 12-1/2-inches square.</u>

Make 1

Block 1

Vintage Stitches
Block Two

Cutting

From **LARGE FLORAL**:
- Cut 1, 6-1/2-inch square

From **BEIGE PRINT #1**:
- Cut 1, 3-1/2 x 44-inch strip. From strip cut:
  8, 3-1/2-inch squares

From **DARK ROSE PRINT**:
- Cut 1, 3-1/2 x 44-inch strip. From strip cut:
  4, 3-1/2 x 6-1/2-inch rectangles
- Cut 1, 1-1/2 x 44-inch strip. From strip cut:
  1, 1-1/2 x 14-inch strip
  1, 1-1/2 x 8-inch strip

From **GREEN PRINT**:
- Cut 1, 2-1/2 x 14-inch strip
- Cut 1, 1-1/2 x 44-inch strip. From strip cut:
  2, 1-1/2 x 8-inch strips

Piecing

Step 1 With right sides together, position a 3-1/2-inch **BEIGE #1** square on the corner of a 3-1/2 x 6-1/2-inch **DARK ROSE** rectangle. Draw diagonal line on square; stitch on line, trim, and press. Repeat this process at opposite corner of rectangle. Make 4 units. Sew units to top/bottom edges of the 6-1/2-inch **LARGE FLORAL** square; press.

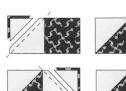

Make 4

Make 1

Step 2 Aligning long raw edges, sew together 1-1/2 x 14-inch **DARK ROSE** strip and 2-1/2 x 14-inch **GREEN** strip; press. Cut strip set into segments.

*Crosscut 8,
1-1/2 inch wide segments*

Step 3 Aligning long raw edges, sew 1-1/2 x 8-inch **GREEN** strips to top/bottom edges of 1-1/2 x 8-inch **DARK ROSE** strip; press. Cut strip set into segments.

*Crosscut 4,
1-1/2-inch wide segments*

Step 4 Sew Step 2 segments to top/bottom edges of Step 3 segments; press. At this point each unit should measure 3-1/2-inches square.

Make 4

Step 5 Sew Step 4 units to both ends of remaining Step 1 units; press. Sew the units to side edges of the **LARGE FLORAL** square unit; press. At this point the block should measure 12-1/2-inches square.

Make 1
Block 2

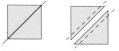
Vintage Stitches

Block Three

Cutting

From **LARGE FLORAL**:
- Cut 1, 6-1/2-inch square

From **YELLOW FLORAL**:
- Cut 2, 4-1/4-inch squares
- Cut 2, 3-7/8-inch squares

From **BEIGE PRINT #1**:
- Cut 2, 4-1/4-inch squares
- Cut 2, 3-7/8-inch squares

From **BLUE/GREEN PRINT**:
- Cut 4, 3-7/8-inch squares

Piecing

Step 1 With right sides together, layer 3-7/8-inch **YELLOW FLORAL** and **BEIGE #1** squares in pairs. Press together, but do not sew. Cut layered squares in half diagonally to make 4 sets of triangles. Stitch 1/4-inch from diagonal edge of each set of triangles; press. Set the triangle-pieced squares aside to be used for corner squares.

3-7/8" squares   *Make 4, 3-1/2-inch triangle-pieced squares*

Step 2 With right sides together, layer 4-1/4-inch **YELLOW FLORAL** and **BEIGE #1** squares in pairs. Press together, but do not sew. Cut layered squares in half diagonally to make 4 sets of triangles. Stitch 1/4-inch from diagonal edge of each set of triangles; press.

4-1/4" squares   *Make 4, 3-7/8-inch triangle-pieced squares*

Step 3 With right sides together, layer Step 2, <u>3-7/8-inch triangle-pieced squares</u> on the 3-7/8-inch **BLUE/GREEN** squares. Press together but do not sew. Cut layered squares in half diagonally to make 8 sets of triangles. Stitch 1/4-inch from diagonal edge of each set of triangles; press.

Make 4 each, 3-1/2-inch triangle-pieced squares

Step 4 Referring to diagrams for placement, sew together Step 3 units in pairs; press. Make 2 A Units and 2 B Units. <u>At this point each unit should measure 3-1/2 x 6-1/2-inches.</u>

Make 2, A Units

Make 2, B Units

Step 5 Sew A Units to top/bottom edges of the 6-1/2-inch **LARGE FLORAL** square; press. <u>At this point the unit should measure 6-1/2 x 12-1/2-inches.</u>

Step 6 Sew Step 1, <u>3-1/2-inch triangle-pieced squares</u> (corner squares) to both ends of B Units; press. Sew the units to side edges of the **LARGE FLORAL** square unit; press. <u>At this point the block should measure 12-1/2-inches square.</u>

A Unit

A Unit
Make 1

Make 1
Block 3

Vintage Stitches
Block Four

Cutting

From **LARGE FLORAL**:
- Cut 1, 6-1/2-inch square

From **GREEN PRINT**:
- Cut 1, 2-1/2 x 44-inch strip. From strip cut:
  4, 2-1/2-inch squares
  2, 1-1/2 x 6-1/2-inch rectangles
  2, 1-1/2 x 8-1/2-inch rectangles

From **BEIGE PRINT #1**:
- Cut 2, 1-1/2 x 44-inch strips. From strips cut:
  32, 1-1/2-inch squares

From **BLUE PRINT**:
- Cut 1, 2-1/2 x 44-inch strip. From strip cut:
  16, 2-1/2-inch squares

Piecing

Step 1   Sew 1-1/2 x 6-1/2-inch **GREEN** rectangles to top/bottom edges of the 6-1/2-inch **LARGE FLORAL** square; press. Sew 1-1/2 x 8-1/2-inch **GREEN** rectangles to side edges of square; press. <u>At this point the unit should measure 8-1/2-inches square.</u>

Make 1

Step 2   With right sides together, position a 1-1/2-inch **BEIGE #1** square on the corner of a 2-1/2-inch **BLUE** square. Draw diagonal line on **BEIGE #1** square; stitch on line, trim, and press. Repeat this process at opposite corner of blue square.

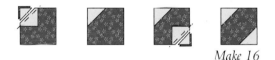

Make 16

Step 3   Sew together 4 of the Step 2 units; press. Make 4 units; press. <u>At this point each unit should measure 2-1/2 x 8 1/2-inches.</u>

Make 4

Step 4   Sew Step 3 units to top/bottom edges of the **LARGE FLORAL** square unit; press. Sew 2-1/2-inch **GREEN** squares to both side edges of remaining Step 3 units; press. Sew the units to side edges of **LARGE FLORAL** square unit; press. <u>At this point the block should measure 12-1/2-inches square.</u>

Make 1
Block 4

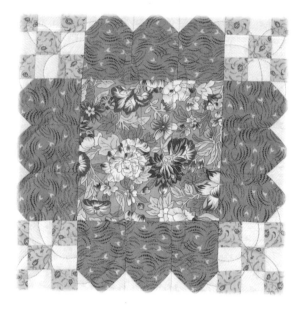

Vintage Stitches
Block Five

Cutting

From **LARGE FLORAL**:
- Cut 1, 6-1/2-inch square

From **BEIGE PRINT #1**:
- Cut 2, 1-1/2 x 44-inch strips. From strips cut: 40, 1-1/2-inch squares

From **LIGHT TEAL PRINT**:
- Cut 1, 2-1/2 x 44-inch strip. From strip cut: 12, 2-1/2 x 3-1/2-inch rectangles

From **LIGHT PINK PRINT**:
- Cut 1, 1-1/2 x 44-inch strip. From strip cut: 20, 1-1/2-inch squares

Piecing

Step 1 With right sides together, position a 1-1/2-inch **BEIGE #1** square on upper left corner of a 2-1/2 x 3-1/2-inch **LIGHT TEAL** rectangle. Draw diagonal line on square; stitch on line, trim, and press. Repeat this process at upper right corner of rectangle.

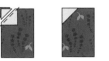

Make 12

Step 2 Sew together 3 of the Step 1 units; press. Make 4 units. <u>At this point each unit should measure 3-1/2 x 6-1/2-inches.</u> Sew units to top/bottom edges of the 6-1/2-inch **LARGE FLORAL** square; press.

Make 4

Make 1

Step 3 To make each 9-patch corner square, sew together 5 of the 1-1/2-inch **LIGHT PINK** squares and 4 of the 1-1/2-inch **BEIGE #1** squares; press. <u>At this point each 9-patch corner square should measure 3-1/2-inches square.</u>

Make 4, 9-patch corner squares

Step 4 Sew 9-patch corner squares to both ends of remaining Step 2 units; press. Sew the units to side edges of the **LARGE FLORAL** square unit; press. <u>At this point the block should measure 12-1/2-inches square.</u>

Make 1
Block 5

Vintage Stitches
Block Six

Cutting

From **LARGE FLORAL**:
- Cut 1, 6-1/2-inch square

From **PINK PRINT**:
- Cut 1, 1-1/2 x 44-inch strip. From strip cut:
  2, 1-1/2 x 8-1/2-inch rectangles
  2, 1-1/2 x 6-1/2-inch rectangles

From **BLUE FLORAL**:
- Cut 1, 2-1/2 x 44-inch strip. From strip cut:
  16, 2-1/2-inch squares

From **BEIGE PRINT #1**:
- Cut 2, 2-1/2 x 44-inch strips. From strips cut:
  8, 2-1/2 x 4-1/2-inch rectangles
  4, 2-1/2-inches squares

Piecing

Step 1   Sew 1-1/2 x 6-1/2-inch **PINK** rectangles to top/bottom edges of the 6-1/2-inch **LARGE FLORAL** square; press. Sew 1-1/2 x 8-1/2-inch **PINK** rectangles to side edges of square; press. <u>At this point the unit should measure 8-1/2-inches square.</u>

Make 1

Step 2   With right sides together, position a 2-1/2-inch **BLUE FLORAL** square on the corner of a 2-1/2 x 4-1/2-inch **BEIGE #1** rectangle. Draw diagonal line on square; stitch on line, trim, and press. Repeat this process at opposite corner of rectangle.

Make 8

Step 3   Sew Step 2 units together in pairs; press. <u>At this point each unit should measure 2-1/2 x 8-1/2-inches.</u>

Make 1

Step 4   Sew Step 3 units to top/bottom edges of the **LARGE FLORAL** square unit; press. Sew 2-1/2-inch **BEIGE #1** squares to both ends of remaining Step 3 units; press. Sew units to side edges of the **LARGE FLORAL** square unit; press. <u>At this point the block should measure 12-1/2-inches square.</u>

Make 1
Block 6

Vintage Stitches
Block Seven

Cutting

From **LARGE FLORAL**:
• Cut 1, 6-1/2-inch square

From **DARK GREEN PRINT**:
• Cut 2, 1-1/2 x 44-inch strips
• Cut 1, 1-1/2 x 14-inch strip

From **BEIGE PRINT #1**:
• Cut 1, 1-1/2 x 44-inch strip
• Cut 2 more 1-1/2 x 44-inch strips. From strips cut:
  2, 1-1/2 x 14-inch strips
  8, 1-1/2 x 2-1/2-inch rectangles
  16, 1-1/2-inch squares

From **LIGHT BLUE PRINT**:
• Cut 1, 1-1/2 x 44-inch strip. From strip cut:
  4, 1-1/2 x 3-1/2-inch rectangles
  8, 1-1/2-inch squares

Piecing

Step 1 Aligning long raw edges, sew 1-1/2 x 44-inch **DARK GREEN** strips to top/bottom edges of 1-1/2 x 44-inch **BEIGE #1** strip; press. Cut strip set into segments.

Crosscut 4, 2-1/2-inch wide segments *Crosscut 8, 1-1/2-inch wide segments*

Step 2 Aligning long raw edges, sew 1-1/2 x 14-inch **BEIGE #1** strips to top/bottom edges of 1-1/2 x 14-inch **DARK GREEN** strip; press. Cut strip set into segments.

Crosscut 8, 1-1/2-inch wide segments

Step 3 Referring to diagram for placement, sew together Step 1 and Step 2 segments; press. At this point each unit should measure 3-1/2 x 6-1/2-inches.

Make 4

Step 4 Sew Step 3 units to top/bottom edges of the 6-1/2-inch **LARGE FLORAL** square; press.

Make 1

Step 5 With right sides together, position a 1-1/2-inch **LIGHT BLUE** square on right corner of a 1-1/2 x 2-1/2-inch **BEIGE #1** rectangle. Draw diagonal line on square; stitch on line, trim, and press. Sew 1-1/2-inch **BEIGE #1** square to right edge of unit; press. At this point each unit should measure 1-1/2 x 3-1/2-inches.

 *Make 8*

Step 6 With right sides together, position a 1-1/2-inch **BEIGE #1** square on the corner of a 1-1/2 x 3-1/2-inch **LIGHT BLUE** rectangle. Draw diagonal line on square; stitch on line, trim, and press. Repeat this process at opposite corner of rectangle.

  Make 4

Step 7 Sew the Step 5 units to top/bottom edges of each Step 6 unit; press. At this point each star unit should measure 3-1/2-inches square.

Make 4

Step 8 Sew star units to both ends of remaining Step 3 units; press. Sew units to side edges of the **LARGE FLORAL** square unit; press. At this point the block should measure 12-1/2-inches square.

Make 1
Block 7

Vintage Stitches
Block Eight

Cutting

From **LARGE FLORAL**:
• Cut 1, 6-1/2-inch square

From **GOLD PRINT**:
• Cut 3, 4-1/4-inch squares

From **BEIGE PRINT #1**:
• Cut 6, 4-1/4-inch squares

From **PINK/YELLOW PRINT**:
• Cut 3, 4-1/4-inch squares

Piecing

Step 1   To make hourglass units, with right sides together, layer the 4-1/4-inch **GOLD** squares and 3 of the 4-1/4-inch **BEIGE #1** squares in pairs. Press together, but do not sew. Cut layered squares diagonally into quarters to make 12 sets of triangles. Stitch along bias edge of layered triangles as shown; press. Sew triangle sets together in pairs to make hourglass units; press. At this point each hourglass unit should measure 3-1/2-inches square.

Make 12
triangle sets

Make 6
hourglass units

Step 2   To make hourglass units, with right sides together, layer the 4-1/4-inch **PINK/YELLOW** squares and 3 of the 4-1/4-inch **BEIGE #1** squares in pairs. Press together, but do not sew. Cut layered squares diagonally into quarters to make 12 sets of triangles. Stitch along bias edge of layered triangles as shown; press. Sew triangle sets together in pairs to make hourglass units; press. At this point each hourglass unit should measure 3-1/2-inches square.

Bias edges

Make 12
triangle sets

Make 6
hourglass units

Step 3   Sew together Step 1 and Step 2 hourglass units in pairs; press. At this point each unit should measure 3-1/2 x 6-1/2-inches.

Make 2
Unit A

Make 4
Unit B

Step 4   Sew the Step 3 A Units to top/bottom edges of the 6-1/2-inch **LARGE FLORAL** square; press.

Make 1

Step 5   Sew the Step 3 B Units together in pairs; press. At this point each unit should measure 3-1/2 x 12-1/2-inches. Sew the units to side edges of the **LARGE FLORAL** square unit; press. At this point the block should measure 12-1/2-inches square.

Make 1
Block 8

Vintage Stitches
Block Nine

Cutting

From **LARGE FLORAL**:
  • Cut 1, 6-1/2-inch square

From **YELLOW PRINT**:
  • Cut 1, 2 x 44-inch strip. From strip cut:
    8, 2-inch squares
    1, 1-1/2 x 16-inch strip
  • Cut 1, 1-1/2 x 44-inch strip. From strip cut:
    2, 1-1/2 x 16-inch strips

From **BEIGE PRINT #1**:
  • Cut 2, 1-1/2 x 44-inch strips. From strips cut:
    3, 1-1/2 x 16-inch strips

From **GREEN PRINT**:
  • Cut 1, 2 x 44-inch strip. From strip cut:
    8, 2 x 3-1/2-inch rectangles

Piecing

Step 1 Aligning long raw edges, sew 1-1/2 x 16-inch **YELLOW** strips to top/bottom edges of a 1-1/2 x 16-inch **BEIGE #1** strip; press. Cut strip set into segments.

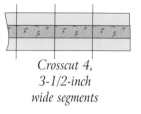

*Crosscut 4,
3-1/2-inch
wide segments*

Step 2 Aligning long raw edges, sew 1-1/2 x 16-inch **BEIGE #1** strips to top/bottom edges of a 1-1/2 x 16-inch **YELLOW** strip; press. Cut strip set into segments.

*Crosscut 4,
3-1/2-inch
wide segments*

Step 3 With right sides together, position a 2-inch **YELLOW** square on the corner of a 2 x 3-1/2-inch **GREEN** rectangle. Draw diagonal line on square; stitch on line, trim, and press. Make 4 A Units. Repeat this process changing the direction of stitching line to make 4 B Units. Sew A and B Units together in pairs; press. <u>At this point each unit should measure 3-1/2-inches square.</u>

Make 4, Unit A

Make 4, Unit B

Make 4

Step 4 Sew Step 1 segments to left edge of Step 3 A/B Units; press. <u>At this point each unit should measure 3-1/2 x 6-1/2-inches.</u>

*Step 1   Step 3
Make 4*

Step 5 Sew Step 4 units to top/bottom edges of the 6-1/2-inch **LARGE FLORAL** square; press. <u>At this point the unit should measure 6-1/2 x 12-1/2-inches.</u>

Make 1

Step 6 Sew Step 2 segments to both ends of remaining Step 4 units; press. Sew units to side edges of the **LARGE FLORAL** square; press. <u>At this point the block should measure 12-1/2-inches square.</u>

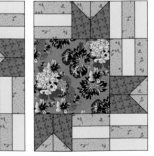

Make 1

Block 9

Vintage Stitches
Block Ten

Cutting

From **LARGE FLORAL**:
- Cut 1, 6-1/2-inch square

From **BROWN/GREEN PRINT**:
- Cut 1, 3-7/8 x 44-inch strip. From strip cut:
  4, 3-7/8-inch squares
  4, 2-1/2-inch squares

From **BEIGE PRINT #1**:
- Cut 1, 3-7/8 x 44-inch strip. From strip cut:
  4, 3-7/8-inch squares
  8, 1-1/2-inch squares

From **ROSE/BROWN PRINT**:
- Cut 1, 3-1/2 x 44-inch strip. From strip cut:
  4, 3-1/2 x 6-1/2-inch rectangles
  4, 1-1/2 x 2-1/2-inch rectangles
- Cut 1, 1-1/2 x 16-inch strip. From strip cut:
  4, 1-1/2 x 3-1/2-inch rectangles

Piecing

Step 1 With right sides together, layer together 3-7/8-inch **BEIGE #1** and **BROWN/GREEN** squares in pairs. Press together, but do not sew. Cut each layered square in half

diagonally to make 8 sets of triangles. Stitch 1/4-inch from diagonal edge of each set of triangles; press.

Make 8, 3-1/2-inch triangle-pieced squares

Step 2 With right sides together, position a Step 1 triangle-pieced square on the corner of a 3-1/2 x 6-1/2-inch **ROSE/BROWN** rectangle; notice the direction of seam line. Draw diagonal line on the triangle-pieced square; stitch on line, trim, and press. Repeat this process at opposite corner of rectangle.

Make 4

Step 3 Sew Step 2 units to top/bottom edges of the 6-1/2-inch **LARGE FLORAL** square; press. At this point the unit should measure 6-1/2 x 12-1/2-inches.

Step 4 With right sides together, position a 1-1/2-inch **BEIGE #1** square on upper corner of a 1-1/2 x 2-1/2-inch **ROSE/BROWN** rectangle. Draw diagonal line on square; stitch on line, trim, and press. Make 4 units. Sew units to right side edge of each 2-1/2-inch **BROWN/GREEN** square; press.

Make 1

Make 4 *Make 4*

Step 5 With right sides together, position a 1-1/2-inch **BEIGE #1** square on left corner of a 1-1/2 x 3-1/2-inch **ROSE/BROWN** rectangle. Draw diagonal line on square; stitch on line, trim, and press. Make 4 units. Sew units to bottom edge of each Step 4 unit; press.

Make 4

Make 4

Step 6 Sew Step 5 units to both ends of remaining Step 2 units; press. Sew units to side edges of the **LARGE FLORAL** square unit; press. At this point the block should measure 12-1/2-inches square.

Make 1

Block 10   21

Vintage Stitches
Block Eleven

Cutting

From **LARGE FLORAL**:
• Cut 1, 6-1/2-inch square

From **TONAL ROSE PRINT**:
• Cut 1, 2-1/2 x 44-inch strip. From strip cut:
4, 2-1/2-inch squares
1, 1-7/8 x 18-inch strip

From **BEIGE PRINT #1**:
• Cut 1, 2-1/2 x 44-inch strip. From strip cut:
1, 2-1/2 x 30-inch strip
4, 1-1/2-inch squares
• Cut 1, 1-7/8 x 18-inch strip

From **GREEN PRINT**:
• Cut 1, 1-1/2 x 30-inch strip

Piecing

Step 1 With right sides together, layer together 1-7/8 x 18-inch **BEIGE #1** and **TONAL ROSE** strips. Press together, but do not sew. Cut layered strip into squares. Cut each layered square in half diagonally to make 16 sets of triangles. Stitch 1/4-inch from diagonal edge of each set of triangles; press.

Crosscut 8, 1-7/8-inch squares

 Make 16, 1-1/2-inch triangle-pieced squares

Step 2 Sew Step 1 triangle-pieced squares together in pairs to make units; press.

Make 4, A Unit   *Make 4, B Unit*

Step 3 Sew the A Units to bottom edge of each 2-1/2-inch **TONAL ROSE** square; press. Sew the 1-1/2-inch **BEIGE #1** squares to bottom edge of each B Unit; press.

Make 4 A Unit   *Make 4 B Unit*

Step 4 Sew B Units to right edge of A Units; press. <u>At this point each unit should measure 3-1/2-inches square.</u>

Make 4

Step 5 Aligning long edges, sew together 1-1/2 x 30-inch **GREEN** strip and 2-1/2 x 30-inch **BEIGE #1** strip; press. Cut strip set into segments.

Crosscut 8, 3-1/2-inch wide segments

Step 6 Sew Step 5 segments and Step 4 units together in pairs; press. <u>At this point each unit should measure 3-1/2 x 6-1/2-inches.</u>

Step 5 Step 4

Make 4

Step 7 Sew Step 6 units to top/bottom edges of the 6-1/2-inch **LARGE FLORAL** square; press. <u>At this point the unit should measure 6-1/2 x 12-1/2-inches.</u>

Make 1

Step 8 Sew remaining Step 5 segments to both ends of remaining Step 6 units; press. Sew units to side edges of the **LARGE FLORAL** square unit; press. <u>At this point the block should measure 12-1/2-inches square.</u>

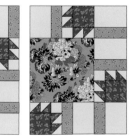

Make 1

Block 11

Vintage Stitches
Block Twelve

Cutting

From **LARGE FLORAL**:
- Cut 1, 6-1/2-inch square

From **BEIGE PRINT #1**:
- Cut 1, 4-1/4 x 44-inch strip. From strip cut:
  4, 4-1/4-inch squares
  1, 1-7/8 x 18-inch strip
  4, 1-1/2-inch squares

From **LIGHT ROSE PRINT**:
- Cut 1, 4-1/4 x 44-inch strip. From strip cut:
  4, 4-1/4-inch squares
  4, 2-1/2-inch squares

From **BROWN PRINT**:
- Cut 1, 1-7/8 x 18-inch strip

Piecing

Step 1 To make hourglass units, with right sides together, layer the 4-1/4-inch **BEIGE #1** and **LIGHT ROSE** squares in pairs. Press together, but do not sew. Cut layered squares diagonally into quarters to make 16 sets of triangles. Stitch along bias edge of layered triangles as shown; press. Sew triangle sets together in pairs to make hourglass units; press.

At this point each hourglass unit should measure 3-1/2-inches square.

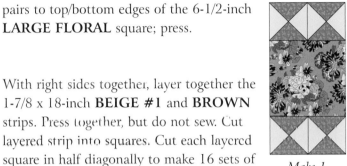

Bias edges

Make 16 triangle sets

Make 8 hourglass units

Step 2 Sew hourglass units together in pairs; press. At this point each pair should measure 3-1/2 x 6-1/2-inches. Sew the pairs to top/bottom edges of the 6-1/2-inch **LARGE FLORAL** square; press.

Make 4 pairs

Make 1

Step 3 With right sides together, layer together the 1-7/8 x 18-inch **BEIGE #1** and **BROWN** strips. Press together, but do not sew. Cut layered strip into squares. Cut each layered square in half diagonally to make 16 sets of triangles. Stitch 1/4-inch from diagonal edge of each set of triangles; press.

Crosscut 8, 1-7/8-inch squares

Make 16, 1-1/2-inch triangle-pieced squares

Step 4 Sew triangle-pieced squares together in pairs to make units; press.

Make 4 A Unit   *Make 4 B Unit*

Step 5 Sew the A Units to bottom edge of each 2-1/2-inch **LIGHT ROSE** square; press. Sew the 1-1/2-inch **BEIGE #1** squares to bottom edge of each B Unit; press.

Make 4 A Unit   *Make 4 B Unit*

Step 6 Sew B Units to right edge of A Units; press. At this point each unit should measure 3-1/2-inches square.

Make 4

Step 7 Sew Step 6 units to both ends of remaining Step 2 pairs; press. Sew units to side edges of the **LARGE FLORAL** square unit; press. At this point the block should measure 12-1/2-inches square.

Make 1

Block 12

Block Borders

Cutting

From **BROWN PRINT**:
- Cut 17, 1-1/2 x 44-inch strips. From strips cut:
  24, 1-1/2 x 14-1/2-inch inner block border strips
  24, 1-1/2 x 12-1/2-inch inner block border strips

From **BEIGE PRINT #1**:
- Cut 24, 1-1/2 x 44-inch strips. From strips cut:
  24, 1-1/2 x 16-1/2-inch strips
  24, 1-1/2 x 14-1/2-inch strips

Attaching Block Borders

Step 1   Make all 12 of the 12-1/2-inch pieced blocks.

Step 2   Sew 1-1/2 x 12-1/2-inch **BROWN** strips to top/bottom edges of each pieced block; press. Sew 1-1/2 x 14-1/2-inch **BROWN** strips to side edges of each pieced block; press.

Step 3   Sew 1-1/2 x 14-1/2-inch **BEIGE #1** strips to top/bottom edges of each pieced block; press. Sew 1-1/2 x 16-1/2-inch **BEIGE #1** strips to side edges of each pieced block; press. At this point each pieced block should measure 16-1/2-inches square.

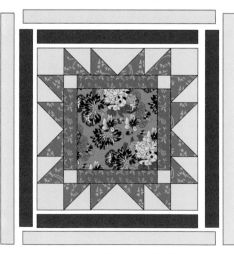

Make 12 bordered blocks

Quilt Center

Cutting

From **BROWN PRINT**—cut on crosswise grain:
- Cut 4, 2-1/2 x 44-inch strips. From strips cut:
  8, 2-1/2 x 16-1/2-inch vertical lattice segments
- Cut 12 more 2-1/2 x 44-inch horizontal lattice & inner border strips. Diagonally piece as needed.

Quilt Center Assembly

Step 1   Referring to quilt diagram for block placement, sew together 3 blocks and 2 of the 2-1/2 x 16-1/2-inch **BROWN** lattice segments. Press seam allowances toward lattice segments. Make 4 block rows. At this point each block row should measure 16-1/2 x 52-1/2-inches.

Step 2   Cut the 2-1/2-inch wide **BROWN** vertical lattice/inner border strips into 5, 2-1/2 x 52-1/2-inch horizontal strips (or to the length of the block rows).

Step 3   Sew together the block rows and the 5, 2-1/2-inch wide **BROWN** lattice & top/bottom inner border strips; press. At this point the quilt center should measure 52-1/2 x 74-1/2-inches.

Step 4   Cut the 2-1/2-inch wide **BROWN** inner border strips into 2, 2-1/2 x 74-1/2-inch side border strips (or to the length of the quilt top). Attach side border strips to quilt center; press.

Quilt Center Assembly Diagram

Flying Geese Border

Cutting

From **GREEN PRINT**:
• Cut 16, 2-1/2 x 44-inch strips. From strips cut:
   138, 2-1/2 x 4-1/2-inch rectangles

From **BEIGE PRINT #2**:
• Cut 18, 2-1/2 x 44-inch strips. From strips cut:
   276, 2-1/2-inch squares

Piecing

Step 1 With right sides together, layer a 2-1/2-inch
BEIGE #2 square on the corner of a
2-1/2 x 4-1/2-inch **GREEN** rectangle. Draw

diagonal line on square; stitch on line, trim,
and press. Repeat this process at opposite end
of rectangle.

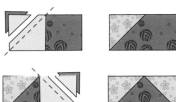

Make 138

Step 2 For top/bottom flying geese borders, sew
28 flying geese units together; press.
At this point each border should measure
4-1/2 x 56-1/2-inches. Sew flying geese borders
to top/bottom edges of quilt center; press.

Step 3 For side flying geese borders, sew 41 flying
geese units together; press. At this point each
border should measure 4-1/2 x 82-1/2-inches.
Sew flying geese borders to side edges of quilt
center; press. At this point quilt center should
measure 64-1/2 x 82-1/2-inches.

Borders
Middle & Outer

*Note: Yardage given allows for middle border
strips to be cut on crosswise grain. Diagonally
piece strips as needed, referring to **Diagonal Piecing**
instructions on page 154. Yardage given allows for wide
outer border strips to be cut on lengthwise grain (a couple
extra inches are allowed for trimming). Cutting wide
border strips lengthwise will eliminate the need for piecing.
Read through **Borders** on page 153 for general
instructions on adding borders.*

Cutting

From **BROWN PRINT**—cut on crosswise grain:
• Cut 9, 4-1/2 x 44-inch middle border strips

From **LARGE FLORAL**—cut on lengthwise grain:
• Cut 2, 10-1/2 x 117-inch side border strips
• Cut 2, 10-1/2 x 76-inch top/bottom border strips

Attaching Borders

Step 1 Attach 4-1/2-inch wide **BROWN** middle border strips.

Step 2 Attach 10-1/2-inch wide **LARGE FLORAL** outer border strips.

Putting It All Together

If using 108-inch wide backing fabric, simply trim backing and batting so they are 6-inches larger than quilt top.

Note: If using 44-inch wide backing fabric, cut the 8-1/4 yard length of backing fabric in thirds crosswise to make 3, 2-3/4 yard lengths. Refer to Finishing the Quilt on page 154 for complete instructions.

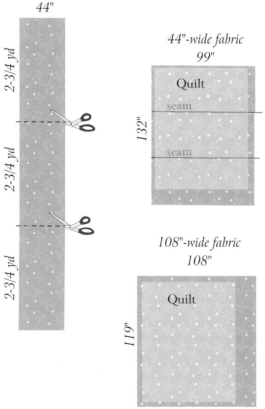

Finished Back Diagram

Quilting Suggestions:

- Pieced blocks
  TB 87—11-1/2" Heart Swirl

- **BROWN** 1" borders nothing

- **CREAM** 1" borders stipple

- **BROWN** 2" border
  TB 67—1-1/2" Heart Chain

- Flying Geese stipple in **BEIGE**

- **BROWN** 4" border
  TB 65—3-1/2" Nordic Scroll

- **LARGE FLORAL** outer border—meander

Thimbleberries *quilt stencils by Quilting Creations International are available at your local quilt shop or visit www.quiltingcreations.com.*

Binding

Cutting

From **GREEN PRINT**:
- Cut 11, 2-3/4 x 44-inch strips

Sew binding to quilt using a 3/8-inch seam allowance. This measurement will produce a 1/2-inch wide finished double binding. Refer to **Binding** and **Diagonal Piecing** on page 154 for complete instructions.

Vintage Stitches Quilt

92 x 110-inches

VINTAGE STITCHES PILLOW

18-inches square without ruffles

Fabrics & Supplies

1/3 yard **BEIGE PRINT** for center square, pillow top

7/8 yard **YELLOW FLORAL**
or pillow top, pillow back

1/8 yard **BLUE/GREEN PRINT** for pillow top

1/8 yard **BROWN PRINT** inner border

1/2 yard **LARGE FLORAL** for outer border, ruffle

24-inch square **BEIGE PRINT** for pillow top lining

quilt batting, at least 24-inches square

brown embroidery floss
(The Gentle Art—www.thegentleart.com—
Maple Syrup)

embroidery hoop, embroidery needle

18-inch pillow form

Pillow Top

Cutting

From **BEIGE PRINT**:
- Cut 1, 11-inch square. The square will be trimmed to 6-1/2-inches square when the embroidery is complete.
- Cut 2, 4-1/4-inch squares
- Cut 2, 3-7/8-inch squares

From **YELLOW FLORAL**:
- Cut 2, 4-1/4-inch squares
- Cut 2, 3-7/8-inch squares

From **BLUE/GREEN PRINT**:
- Cut 4, 3-7/8-inch squares

Embroider the Center Square

Step 1   Transfer embroidery design on page 32 onto 11-inch **BEIGE** center square. To do so, make a copy of the embroidery design. Tape the design to a window. Position the **BEIGE** square of fabric over the design; tape in place. Using a #2 mechanical pencil, trace the design onto the fabric. Remove the fabric and design from window.

Step 2   With 3 strands of embroidery floss, stitch the design with the outline stitch, straight stitch, and lazy daisy stitch.

Straight stitch   *Outline/stem stitch*   *Lazy daisy stitch*

Step 3   Trim **EMBROIDERED** square to 6-1/2-inches square.

Piecing

Step 1   With right sides together, layer 3-7/8-inch **YELLOW FLORAL** and **BEIGE** squares. Press together, but do not sew. Cut layered squares in half diagonally to make 4 sets of triangles. Stitch 1/4-inch from diagonal edge of each set of triangles; press. Set the triangle-pieced squares aside to be used for corner squares.

3-7/8" squares

Make 4, 3-1/2-inch triangle-pieced squares

Step 2 With right sides together, layer 4-1/4-inch **YELLOW FLORAL** and **BEIGE** squares. Press together, but do not sew. Cut layered squares in half diagonally to make 4 sets of triangles. Stitch 1/4-inch from diagonal edge of each set of triangles; press.

4-1/4" squares

Make 4, 3-7/8-inch triangle-pieced squares

Step 3 With right sides together, layer Step 2, 3-7/8-inch triangle-pieced squares on the 3-7/8-inch **BLUE/GREEN** squares. Press together but do not sew. Cut layered squares in half diagonally to make 8 sets of triangles. Stitch 1/4-inch from diagonal edge of each set of triangles; press.

Make 4, 3-1/2-inch triangle-pieced squares

Make 4, 3-1/2-inch triangle-pieced squares

Step 4 Referring to diagrams for placement, sew together Step 3 units in pairs; press. Make 2 A Units and 2 B Units. At this point each unit should measure 3-1/2 x 6-1/2-inches.

Make 2, A Units   *Make 2, B Units*

Step 5 Sew A Units to top/bottom edges of the 6-1/2-inch **EMBROIDERED** square; press. At this point the unit should measure 6-1/2 x 12-1/2-inches.

Step 6 Sew Step 1, 3-1/2-inch triangle-pieced squares (corner squares) to both ends of B Units; press. Sew the units to side edges of the **EMBROIDERED** square unit; press. At this point the block should measure 12-1/2-inches square.

Make 1

Borders

Cutting

From **BROWN PRINT**:
• Cut 2, 1-1/2 x 44-inch strips. From strips cut:
  2, 1-1/2 x 14-1/2-inch inner border strips
  2, 1-1/2 x 12-1/2-inch inner border strips

From **LARGE FLORAL**:
• Cut 2, 2-1/2 x 44-inch strips. From strips cut:
  2, 2-1/2 x 18-1/2-inch outer border strips
  2, 2-1/2 x 14-1/2-inch outer border strips

Attach Borders

Step 1 Sew 1-1/2 x 12-1/2-inch **BROWN** strips to top/bottom edges of pieced block; press. Sew 1-1/2 x 14-1/2-inch **BROWN** strips to side edges of pieced block; press.

Step 2 Sew 2-1/2 x 14-1/2-inch **LARGE FLORAL** strips to top/bottom edges of pieced block; press. Sew 2-1/2 x 18-1/2-inch **LARGE FLORAL** strips to side edges of pieced block; press. At this point pillow top should measure 18-1/2-inches square.

Putting It All Together

Cutting

From **BEIGE** lining and batting:
• Cut 1, 24-inch square from each

Quilt the Pillow Top

Step 1 Layer 24-inch **BEIGE** lining square, batting square, and prepared pillow top facing up.

Step 2 Pin or hand baste layers together and quilt by hand or machine. Trim batting and lining even with pillow top edge (18-1/2-inches square).

Step 3 Hand baste the edges together to prevent them from rippling when the ruffle is sewn to the quilted pillow top.

Ruffle

Cutting

From **LARGE FLORAL**:
• Cut 4, 2-1/2 x 44-inch strips for ruffle

Attach Ruffle

Step 1 Diagonally piece 2-1/2-inch wide **LARGE FLORAL** strips together to make a continuous ruffle strip. Fold strip in half lengthwise, wrong sides together; press. Divide ruffle strip into 4 equal segments; mark quarter points with safety pins.

Step 2 To gather ruffle, position a heavy thread (quilting thread) 1/4-inch in from raw edges of ruffle strip. Thread should be about 200-inches long. Secure one end by stitching across it. Zigzag stitch over thread all the way around ruffle strip, taking care not to sew through thread.

zigzag
secure

Step 3 Divide pillow top edges into 4 equal segments; mark quarter points. With right sides together and raw edges aligned, pin ruffle to pillow top matching quarter points. Pull up gathering stitches until ruffle fits pillow top taking care to allow extra fullness in the ruffle at each corner. Sew ruffle to pillow top using a 1/4-inch seam allowance.

Pillow Back

Cutting

From **YELLOW FLORAL**:
• Cut 1, 25 x 44-inch strip. From strip cut: 2, 18-1/2 x 25-inch rectangles for pillow back

Assemble Pillow Back

Step 1 With wrong sides together, fold pillow back rectangles in half crosswise to make 2, 12-1/2 x 18-1/2-inch double-thick pillow back pieces. Overlap folded edges so pillow back measures 18-1/2-inches square; pin pieces together.

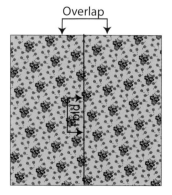
Overlap
Right

Machine baste around entire piece using a 1/4-inch seam allowance to create a single pillow back.

Step 2 With right sides together, layer pillow back and pillow top; pin. The ruffle will be sandwiched between the 2 layers and

turned toward center of pillow at this time. Stitch around outside edges using a 3/8-inch seam allowance.

Step 3 Turn pillow right side out, insert pillow form through back opening, and fluff up ruffle.

Template for center block

Vintage Stitches Pillow

18-inches square without ruffle

Four Seasons

Spring, summer, autumn, winter—
each season brings with it a spirit of change.

What better way to welcome the change than
by creating a charming Thimbleberries® wall quilt.
Whether you begin with the awakening colors of spring
or the pumpkin and wheat colors of autumn's harvest,
you'll discover that your quilts work up quickly—
and oh, so easily— one block at a time.

WINDOW BOX WALL QUILT

40 x 52-inches

Fabrics & Supplies

1/4 yard **BEIGE PRINT** for background

1/3 yard **CHESTNUT FLORAL**
for flower blocks

1/4 yard **ROSE PRINT** for flower blocks

1/8 yard **BLUE FLORAL** for flower blocks

1/4 yard **DARK BLUE PRINT**
for flower blocks

1/8 yard **GREEN PRINT #1** for flower blocks

1/8 yard **GREEN PRINT #2** for flower block

3/8 yard **LIGHT GOLD FLORAL**
for block borders

3/8 yard **MEDIUM GOLD FLORAL**
for block borders

1/4 yard **LIGHT BLUE PRINT**
for inner border

1-1/4 yards **LARGE GREEN FLORAL**
for outer border

1/2 yard **ROSE PRINT** for binding

2-2/3 yards for backing

quilt batting, at least 46 x 58-inches

*Before beginning this project,
read through* **Getting Started** *on page 145.*

Window Box Wall Quilt

Block One

Make 2 blocks

Cutting

From **CHESTNUT FLORAL**:
- Cut 8, 1-1/2-inch squares

From **ROSE PRINT**:
- Cut 8, 2-inch squares

From **BLUE FLORAL**:
- Cut 1, 3-1/2 x 44-inch strip. From strip cut:
  8, 3-1/2-inch squares

From **DARK BLUE PRINT**:
- Cut 3, 1-1/2 x 44-inch strips. From strips cut:
  8, 1-1/2 x 4-1/2-inch rectangles
  8, 1-1/2 x 3-1/2-inch rectangles
  24, 1-1/2-inch squares

From **BEIGE PRINT**:
- Cut 1, 1-1/2 x 44-inch strip. From strip cut:
  24, 1-1/2-inch squares

From **LIGHT GOLD FLORAL**:
- Cut 4, 2-1/2 x 44-inch strips. From strips cut:
  6, 2-1/2 x 12-1/2-inch rectangles
  6, 2-1/2 x 8-1/2-inch rectangles
  6, 2-1/2-inch squares

From **MEDIUM GOLD FLORAL**:
- Cut 4, 2-1/2 x 44-inch strips. From strips cut:
  6, 2-1/2 x 12-1/2-inch rectangles
  6, 2-1/2 x 8-1/2-inch rectangles
  6, 2-1/2-inch squares

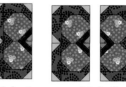

Piecing

Make 2 blocks

Step 1   With right sides together, position a 2-inch **ROSE PRINT** square on the upper left corner of a 3-1/2-inch **BLUE FLORAL** square. Draw diagonal line on **ROSE PRINT** square; stitch on line, trim, and press. Make 8 units. Position a 1-1/2-inch **CHESTNUT FLORAL** square on the **ROSE PRINT** triangle. Draw diagonal line on **CHESTNUT FLORAL** square; stitch on line, trim, and press.

Make 8

Step 2   With right sides together, position 1-1/2-inch **DARK BLUE** squares on the 3 remaining corners of the Step 1 units. Draw diagonal line on **DARK BLUE** squares; stitch on the lines, trim, and press. At this point each unit should measure 3-1/2-inches square.

Make 8

Step 3   With right sides together, position a 1-1/2-inch **BEIGE** square on the right corner of a 1-1/2 x 3-1/2-inch **DARK BLUE** rectangle. Draw diagonal line on square; stitch on line, trim, and press. Make 8 units. Sew the units to right edge of the Step 2 units; press.

Make 8

Step 4   With right sides together, position 1-1/2-inch **BEIGE** squares on the corners of a 1-1/2 x 4-1/2-inch **DARK BLUE** rectangle. Draw diagonal line on squares; stitch, trim, and press. Make 8 units. Sew the units to bottom edge of Step 3 units; press. At this point each unit should measure 4-1/2-inches square.

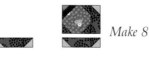

Make 8

Step 5   Sew Step 4 units together in pairs; press. Sew the pairs together to make a flower block; press. At this point each flower block should measure 8-1/2-inches square.

Make 4   *Make 2*

Block Border Assembly

Step 1   With right sides together, position a 2-1/2-inch **MEDIUM GOLD FLORAL** square on the left corner of a 2-1/2 x 12-1/2-inch **LIGHT GOLD FLORAL** rectangle. Draw diagonal line on square; stitch on line, trim, and press.

Make 6

Step 2   With right sides together, position a 2-1/2-inch **LIGHT GOLD FLORAL** square on the left corner of a 2-1/2 x 12-1/2-inch **MEDIUM GOLD FLORAL** rectangle. Draw diagonal line on square, stitch, trim, and press.

Make 6

Step 3   Sew 2-1/2 x 8-1/2-inch **LIGHT GOLD FLORAL** rectangle to top edge of each flower block and sew 2-1/2 x 8-1/2-inch **MEDIUM GOLD FLORAL** rectangle to bottom edge; press.

Step 4   Referring to diagram, sew Step 1 units to right edge of each flower block; press. Sew Step 2 units to the left edge; press. At this point each flower block should measure 12-1/2-inches square.

Make 2, Flower Block 1

Note: *Remaining Block Border units will be added to Flower #2 and #3 blocks.*

Window Box Wall Quilt
Block Two

Make 2 blocks

Cutting

From ROSE PRINT:
• Cut 2, 2-1/2-inch squares

From DARK BLUE PRINT:
• Cut 1, 1-1/2 x 44-inch strip. From strip cut:
  4, 1-1/2 x 4-1/2-inch rectangles
  4, 1-1/2 x 2-1/2-inch rectangles

From CHESTNUT FLORAL:
• Cut 1, 2-1/2 x 44-inch strip. From strip cut:
  16, 2-1/2-inch squares
• Cut 8, 1-1/2-inch squares

From GREEN PRINT #1:
• Cut 8, 2-1/2-inch squares

From BEIGE PRINT:
• Cut 2, 1-1/2 x 44-inch strips. From strips cut:
  48, 1-1/2-inch squares

Piecing

Step 1   With right sides together, position 1-1/2-inch **CHESTNUT FLORAL** squares on the corners of a 1-1/2 x 4-1/2-inch **DARK BLUE** rectangle. Draw diagonal line on squares; stitch on lines, trim, and press.

 *Make 4*

Step 2   Sew 1-1/2 x 2-1/2-inch **DARK BLUE** rectangles to top and bottom edges of a 2-1/2-inch **ROSE PRINT** square; press. Sew Step 1 units to side edges of unit; press. At this point each unit should measure 4-1/2-inches square.

Make 2

Step 3   With right sides together, position a 1-1/2-inch **BEIGE** square on the corner of a 2-1/2-inch **CHESTNUT FLORAL** square. Draw diagonal line on **BEIGE** square; stitch on line, trim, and press toward **BEIGE** triangle. Repeat this process at adjacent corner of **CHESTNUT FLORAL** square; press toward **CHESTNUT FLORAL** square. Make 16 units. Sew the units together in pairs; press. At this point each unit should measure 2-1/2 x 4-1/2-inches.

Make 16   Make 8

Step 4   Position 1-1/2-inch **BEIGE** squares on opposite corners of a 2-1/2-inch **GREEN #1** square. Draw diagonal line on squares; stitch on lines, trim, and press.

 *Make 8*

Step 5   Sew Step 3 units to top and bottom edges of Step 2 units; press. Sew Step 4 units to both edges of remaining Step 3 units; press.

Sew the units to side edges of Step 2 units; press. <u>At this point each flower block should measure 8-1/2-inches square.</u>

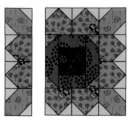

Make 2

Step 6 Sew 2-1/2 x 8-1/2-inch **LIGHT GOLD FLORAL** rectangle to top edge of each flower block and sew 2-1/2 x 8-1/2-inch **MEDIUM GOLD FLORAL** rectangle to bottom edge; press.

Step 7 Referring to diagram, sew prepared **Block Border** units to left and right edges of each flower block; press. <u>At this point each flower block should measure 12-1/2-inches square.</u>

Make 2, Flower Block 2

Note: Remaining **Block Border** units will be added to Flower #3 blocks.

Window Box Wall Quilt
Block Three
Make 2 blocks

Cutting

From DARK BLUE PRINT:
- Cut 1, 1-1/2 x 44-inch strip. From strip cut:
  16, 1-1/2-inch squares

From GREEN PRINT #2:
- Cut 2, 1-1/2 x 44-inch strips. From strips cut:
  24, 1-1/2 x 2-1/2-inch rectangles
  8, 1-1/2-inch squares

From CHESTNUT FLORAL:
- Cut 2, 2-1/2-inch squares

From ROSE PRINT:
- Cut 3, 1-1/2 x 44-inch strips. From strips cut:
  16, 1-1/2 x 3-1/2-inch rectangles
  8, 1-1/2 x 2-1/2-inch rectangles
  8, 1-1/2-inch squares

From BEIGE PRINT:
- Cut 1, 1-1/2 x 44-inch strip. From strip cut:
  8, 1-1/2 x 2-1/2-inch rectangles
  8, 1-1/2-inch squares

Piecing

Step 1 Position a 1-1/2-inch **DARK BLUE** square on the corner of a 1-1/2 x 2-1/2-inch **GREEN #2** rectangle. Draw diagonal line on the square; stitch on the line, trim, and press. Repeat this process at the opposite corner of the rectangle.

 *Make 8*

Step 2 Sew Step 1 units to top and bottom edges of 2-1/2-inch **CHESTNUT FLORAL** squares; press. Sew 1-1/2-inch **GREEN #2** squares to both ends of remaining Step 1 units; press. Sew the units to side edges of this unit; press. At this point each unit should measure 4-1/2-inches square.

 *Make 2*

Step 3 With right sides together, position a 1-1/2 x 2-1/2-inch **GREEN #2** rectangle on the corner of a 1-1/2 x 2-1/2-inch **ROSE** rectangle. Draw diagonal line on **GREEN #2** rectangle; stitch on line, trim, and press. Repeat this process at opposite corner of **ROSE** rectangle. At this point each unit should measure 1-1/2 x 4-1/2-inches.

 *Make 8*

Step 4 Sew Step 3 units to top and bottom edges of Step 2 units; press. Sew 1-1/2-inch **ROSE** squares to both ends of remaining Step 3 units; press. Sew the units to side edges of this unit; press. At this point each unit should measure 6-1/2-inches square.

 *Make 2*

Step 5 With right sides together, position a 1-1/2 x 3-1/2-inch **ROSE** rectangle on the corner of a 1-1/2 x 2-1/2-inch **BEIGE** rectangle. Draw diagonal line on **ROSE** rectangle; stitch on line, trim, and press.

Repeat this process at opposite corner of **BEIGE** rectangle. At this point each unit should measure 1-1/2 x 6-1/2-inches.

 *Make 8*

Step 6 Sew Step 5 units to top and bottom edges of Step 4 units; press. Sew 1-1/2-inch **BEIGE** squares to both ends of remaining Step 5 units; press. Sew the units to side edges of this unit; press. At this point each flower block should measure 8-1/2-inches square.

 *Make 2*

Step 7 Sew 2-1/2 x 8-1/2-inch **LIGHT GOLD FLORAL** rectangle to top edge of each flower block and sew 2-1/2 x 8-1/2-inch **MEDIUM GOLD FLORAL** rectangle to bottom edge; press.

Step 8 Referring to diagram, sew prepared **Block Border** units to left and right edges of each flower block; press. At this point each flower block should measure 12-1/2-inches square.

Make 2, Flower Block 3

Step 9 Referring to quilt diagram, sew flower blocks together in 3 rows with 2 blocks in each row. Press seam allowances in alternating directions by rows so seams will fit snugly together with less bulk. Sew block rows together; press. At this point the quilt center should measure 24-1/2 x 36-1/2 inches.

Borders

*Note: Yardage allows for borders to be cut on crosswise grain. Diagonally piece strips as needed, referring to **Diagonal Piecing** instructions on page 154. Read through **Borders** on page 153 for general instructions on adding borders.*

Cutting

From **LIGHT BLUE PRINT**:
- Cut 4, 1-1/2 x 44-inch inner border strips

From **LARGE GREEN FLORAL**:
- Cut 5, 7-1/2 x 44-inch outer border strips

Attaching the Borders

Step 1   Attach 1-1/2-inch wide **LIGHT BLUE** inner border strips.

Step 2   Attach 7-1/2-inch wide **LARGE GREEN FLORAL** outer border strips.

Putting It All Together

Cut 2-2/3 yard length of backing fabric in half crosswise to make 2, 1-1/3 yard lengths. Refer to *Finishing the Quilt* on page 154 for complete instructions.

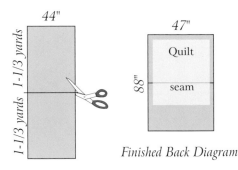

Finished Back Diagram

Quilting Suggestions:

- Block #1
  TB87—11-1/2" Heart Swirl

- Block #2
  TB83—11-1/2" Heart Loop

- Block #3
  TB18—11" Lady Slipper

- **LIGHT BLUE** inner border in-the-ditch

- **LARGE GREEN FLORAL** outer border
  TB43—7" Star Vine Border

Thimbleberries® *quilt stencils by Quilting Creations International are available at your local quilt shop or visit www.quiltingcreations.com.*

Binding

Cutting

From **ROSE PRINT**:
- Cut 5, 2-3/4 x 44-inch strips

Sew binding to quilt using a 3/8-inch seam allowance. This measurement will produce a 1/2-inch wide finished double binding. Refer to *Binding* and *Diagonal Piecing* on page 154 for complete instructions.

Window Box Wall Quilt

40 x 52-inches

SUMMERTIME THROW

54-inches square

Fabrics & Supplies

1/4 yard **RED PRINT #1** for flower blocks

1-1/8 yards **BEIGE PRINT**
for quilt center background /checkerboard border

1/3 yard **GOLD PRINT #1**
for flower blocks, corner squares

1/4 yard **GREEN PRINT** for flower blocks

1/2 yard **BLUE PRINT #1** for sawtooth/inner border

1/3 yard **GOLD PRINT #2** for inner border

1/2 yard **RED PRINT #2** for checkerboard border

1/2 yard **RED PRINT #3** for triangle blocks

1/2 yard **BLUE PRINT #2** for triangle blocks

1/2 yard **BLUE PRINT #3** for border blocks

5/8 yard **BLUE PRINT #1** for binding

3-1/3 yards for backing

quilt batting, at least 60-inches square

*Before beginning this project,
read through* **Getting Started** *on page 145.*

Summertime Throw
Block One

Make 4 blocks

Cutting

From **RED PRINT #1**:
• Cut 2, 2-1/2 x 44-inch strips. From strips cut:
   8, 2-1/2 x 4-1/2-inch rectangles
   8, 2-1/2-inch squares

From **BEIGE PRINT**:
• Cut 1, 4-1/2 x 44-inch strip. From strip cut:
   4, 4-1/2-inch squares.
   Cut squares in half diagonally to make
8 triangles.
• Cut 5, 2-1/2 x 44-inch strips.
   From strips cut:
   2, 2-1/2 x 22-1/2-inch strips
   3, 2-1/2 x 18-1/2-inch strips
   2, 2-1/2 x 8-1/2-inch strips
   8, 2-1/2 x 4-1/2-inch rectangles
• Cut 1, 1-1/2 x 44-inch strip. From strip cut:
   16, 1-1/2-inch squares

4-1/2"

From **GOLD PRINT #1**:
• Cut 1, 2-1/2 x 44-inch strip. From strip cut:
   8, 2-1/2-inch squares

From **GREEN PRINT**:
• Cut 1, 2-1/2 x 44-inch strip. From strip cut:
   16, 2-1/2-inch squares
• Cut 1, 1-1/4 x 44-inch strip. From strip cut:
   4, 1-1/4 x 7-inch stem strips

Piecing

Step 1   Position a 1-1/2-inch **BEIGE** square on the corner of a 2-1/2-inch **RED #1** square. Draw diagonal line on **BEIGE** square; stitch on line. Trim seam allowance to 1/4-inch; press. Sew the unit to right edge of 2-1/2-inch **GOLD #1** square; press. Make 8 units. Sew units together in pairs; press. <u>At this point each unit should measure 4-1/2-inches square.</u>

Make 8   *Make 8*   *Make 4*

Step 2   Position a 1-1/2-inch **BEIGE** square on the upper left corner of a 2-1/2 x 4-1/2-inch **RED #1** rectangle. Draw diagonal line on **BEIGE** square; stitch on line, trim, and press. Position a 2-1/2-inch **GREEN** square on the right corner of this unit. Draw diagonal line on **GREEN** square; stitch on line, trim, and press.

Make 4

Step 3   Position a 1-1/2-inch **BEIGE** square on the lower left corner of a 2-1/2 x 4-1/2-inch **RED #1** rectangle. Draw diagonal line on **BEIGE** square; stitch on line, trim, and press. Position a 2-1/2-inch **GREEN** square on the right corner of this unit. Draw diagonal line on **GREEN** square; stitch on the line, trim, and press.

Make 4

Step 4   Position a 2-1/2-inch **GREEN** square on the corner of a 2-1/2 x 4-1/2-inch **BEIGE** rectangle. Draw diagonal line on **GREEN** square; stitch on line, trim, and press. Make 4 units. Reverse the direction of the drawn sewing line and make another 4 units. Referring to diagrams, sew the units to Step 2 and 3 units; press. <u>At this point each unit should measure 4-1/2-inches square.</u>

Make 4   *Make 4*

Make 4   *Make 4*

Step 5   To make a stem unit, center a **BEIGE** triangle on a 1-1/4 x 7-inch **GREEN** strip and stitch a 1/4-inch seam. Center another **BEIGE** triangle on the opposite edge of the **GREEN** strip; stitch. Press seam allowances toward **GREEN** strip. Trim stem unit so it measures 4-1/2-inches square.

Trim ends

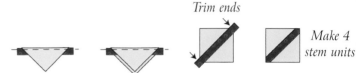

Make 4 stem units

Step 6   Referring to the diagram, sew Step 1, Step 4, and Step 5 units together in rows; press. Sew rows together to make flower blocks; press. <u>At this point each flower block should measure 8-1/2-inches square.</u>

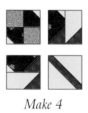

Make 4

Step 7   Referring to quilt center diagram, sew flower blocks to both sides of the 2-1/2 x 8-1/2-inch **BEIGE** strips; press. Sew flower block rows to both sides of a 2-1/2 x 18-1/2-inch **BEIGE** strip; press. Sew remaining 2-1/2 x 18-1/2-inch **BEIGE** strips to top and bottom edges of this unit; press. Sew 2-1/2 x 22-1/2-inch **BEIGE** strips to side edges of the unit; press. <u>At this point the quilt center should measure 22-1/2-inches square.</u>

Quilt Center

Borders

Sawtooth, Inner, & Checkerboard

*Note: Yardage given allows for border strips to be cut on crosswise grain. Diagonally piece strips as needed referring to **Diagonal Piecing** instructions on page 154. Read through **Borders** instructions on page 153 for general instructions on adding borders.*

Cutting

From **BLUE PRINT #1**:
- Cut 2, 2-7/8 x 44-inch strips
- Cut 4, 2-1/2 x 44-inch strips. From 1 of the strips cut:
  4, 2-1/2-inch squares.
  The remaining strips are for first inner border.

From **GOLD PRINT #2**:
- Cut 4, 2-1/2 x 44-inch second inner border strips

From **RED PRINT #2**:
- Cut 5, 2-1/2 x 44-inch strips

From **BEIGE PRINT**:
- Cut 2, 2-7/8 x 44-inch strips
- Cut 5, 2-1/2 x 44-inch strips

Piecing

Step 1 With right sides together, layer 2-7/8 x 44-inch **BLUE #1** and **BEIGE** strips together in pairs. Press together, but do not sew. Cut layered strips into squares. Cut layered squares in half diagonally to make 44 sets of triangles. Stitch 1/4-inch from diagonal edge of each triangle set; press.

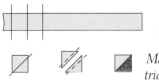

Crosscut 22, 2-7/8-inch squares

Make 44, 2-1/2-inch triangle-pieced squares

Step 2 Referring to diagram, sew 11 of the Step 1 triangle-pieced squares together; press. Make 4 sawtooth strips. <u>At this point each sawtooth strip should measure 2-1/2 x 22-1/2-inches.</u> Sew 2 of the strips to top and bottom edges of quilt center; press. Sew 2-1/2-inch **BLUE #1** squares to both ends of remaining sawtooth strips;

press. Sew the strips to side edges of quilt center; press.

Make 4

Step 3 Attach 2-1/2-inch wide **BLUE #1** first inner border strips.

Step 4 Attach 2-1/2-inch wide **GOLD #2** second inner border strips.

Step 5 Aligning long edges, sew 2-1/2 x 44-inch **RED #2** and **BEIGE** strips together in pairs; press. Refer to the *Hints and Helps for Pressing Strip Sets* on page 152. Make 5 strip sets. Crosscut strip sets into segments.

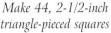

Crosscut 76, 2-1/2-inch wide segments

Step 6 Sew 17 of the Step 5 segments together; press. Make 2 checkerboard borders. <u>At this point each checkerboard border should measure 4-1/2 x 34-1/2-inches.</u> Sew checkerboard borders to top/bottom edges of quilt center; press.

Make 2

Step 7 Sew 21 of the Step 5 segments together; press. Make 2 checkerboard borders. <u>At this point each checkerboard border should measure 4-1/2 x 42-1/2-inches.</u> Sew checkerboard borders to side edges of quilt center; press. <u>At this point the quilt center should measure 42-1/2-inches square.</u>

Make 2

Hourglass Blocks & Pieced Border

Cutting

From **RED PRINT #3**:
- Cut 2, 7-1/4 x 44-inch strips. From strips cut: 8, 7-1/4-inch squares.

From **BLUE PRINT #2**:
- Cut 2, 7-1/4 x 44-inch strips. From strips cut: 8, 7-1/4-inch squares.

From **BLUE PRINT #3**:
- Cut 2, 6-1/2 x 44-inch strips. From strips cut: 12, 6-1/2-inch squares

From **GOLD PRINT #1**:
- Cut 1, 6-1/2 x 44-inch strip. From strip cut: 4, 6-1/2-inch corner squares

Piecing

Step 1 With right sides together, layer the 7-1/4-inch **RED #3** and **BLUE #2** squares in pairs. Press together, but do not sew. Cut layered squares diagonally into quarters to make 34 sets of triangles.

Step 2 Stitch along the bias edge of each triangle set being careful not to stretch the triangles; press. Be sure to sew along the same bias edge of each triangle set. Sew the triangle units together in pairs; press. <u>At this point each hourglass block should measure 6-1/2-inches square</u>.

bias edges

Make 32, triangle units

Make 16, hourglass blocks

Step 3 Sew 4 of the hourglass blocks and 3 of the 6-1/2-inch **BLUE #3** squares together; press. Make 4 pieced border strips. Sew 2 of the pieced border strips to top and bottom edges of quilt center; press.

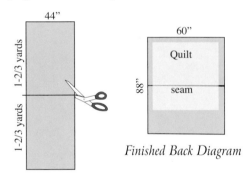

Make 4

Step 4 Sew 6-1/2-inch **GOLD #1** corner squares to both ends of remaining pieced border strips; press. Sew border strips to side edges of quilt center; press.

Putting It All Together

Cut 3-1/3 yard length of backing fabric in half crosswise to make 2, 1-2/3 yard lengths. Refer to **Finishing the Quilt** on page 154 for complete instructions.

44"

1-2/3 yards

1-2/3 yards

60"

Quilt

seam

88"

Finished Back Diagram

Quilting Suggestions:

- Flower blocks—in-the-ditch

- **BEIGE** background (flower, lattice, inner border, sawtooth)—stipple

- **BLUE** sawtooth border-in-the-ditch

- **BLUE** border
  TB93—1-1/2" M-Border

- **GOLD** border
  TB64—1-1/2" Nordic Scroll

- **RED/BEIGE** checkerboard border-in-the-ditch

- Hourglass blocks—in-the-ditch

- **BLUE** and **GOLD** 6" blocks
  TB45—5" Star heart

Thimbleberries® quilt stencils by Quilting Creations International are available at your local quilt shop or visit www.quiltingcreations.com.

Binding

Note: Because of the hourglass blocks in the outer border, sew binding to quilt using a 1/4-inch seam allowance so the tips won't be cut off.

Cutting

From **BLUE PRINT #1:**
• Cut 6, 2-1/2 x 44-inch strips

Sew binding to quilt using 1/4-inch seam allowance. This measurement will produce a 3/8-inch wide finished double binding. Refer to **Binding** and **Diagonal Piecing** on page 154 for complete instructions.

Summertime Throw
54-inches square

AUTUMN GLOW WALL QUILT

42 x 52-inches

Fabrics & Supplies

10-inch square **ORANGE PRINT #1**
for pumpkin block

10-inch square **ORANGE PRINT #2**
for pumpkin block

1/8 yard **GREEN PRINT #1**
for pumpkin stems/maple leaf block

1/8 yard **GREEN PRINT #2** for maple leaf block

1/8 yard **GREEN PRINT #3** for maple leaf block

5/8 yard **BEIGE PRINT** for background

1/3 yard **RUST PRINT** for maple/oak leaf blocks

1/4 yard **GOLD FLORAL** for maple/oak leaf blocks

1/4 yard **GOLD PRINT** for inner border

7/8 yard **BLACK PRINT**
for borders/sawtooth border

1-1/4 yards **RUST/GREEN PRINT**
for outer/sawtooth borders

1/2 yard **BLACK PRINT** for binding

2-2/3 yards for backing

quilt batting, at least 48 x 58-inches

Before beginning this project,
read through **Getting Started** *on page 145.*

Autumn Glow Wall Quilt
Pumpkin & Maple Leaf Sections

Cutting

From *each* **ORANGE PRINT #1** and **#2**:
• Cut 1, 8-1/2-inch square

From **GREEN PRINT #1**:
• Cut 1, 2-7/8 x 44-inch strip. From strip cut:
  1, 2-7/8-inch square
  1, 2-1/2 x 6-1/2-inch rectangle
  1, 2-1/2 x 4-1/2-inch rectangle
  3, 2-1/2-inch squares
  1, 1 x 5-inch rectangle

From **BEIGE PRINT**:
• Cut 1, 2-7/8 x 44-inch strip. From strip cut:
  6, 2-7/8-inch squares
  6, 2-5/8-inch squares.
  Cut squares in half diagonally to make 12 triangles.
• Cut 4, 2-1/2 x 44-inch strips. From strips cut:
  3, 2-1/2 x 10-1/2-inch rectangles
  4, 2-1/2 x 6-1/2-inch rectangles
  2, 2-1/2 x 5-1/2-inch rectangles
  2, 2-1/2 x 3-1/2-inch rectangles
  20, 2-1/2-inch squares

From *each* **GREEN PRINT #2**,
GREEN PRINT #3, and **GOLD FLORAL**:
• Cut 1, 2-7/8 x 44-inch strip. From strip cut:
  1, 2-7/8-inch square
  1, 2-1/2 x 6-1/2-inch rectangle
  1, 2-1/2 x 4-1/2-inch rectangle
  1, 2-1/2-inch square
  1, 1 x 5-inch rectangle

From **RUST PRINT**:
• Cut 2, 2-7/8-inch squares
• Cut 1, 2-1/2 x 44-inch strip. From strip cut:
  2, 2-1/2 x 6-1/2-inch rectangles
  2, 2-1/2 x 4-1/2-inch rectangles
  2, 2-1/2-inch squares
  2, 1 x 5-inch rectangles

Pumpkin Block
Block One

Make 2 blocks

Piecing

Step 1   Position 2-1/2-inch **BEIGE** squares on the 4 corners of the 8-1/2-inch **ORANGE #1** square. Draw diagonal line on **BEIGE** squares; stitch on lines, trim, and press. Repeat using 2-1/2-inch **BEIGE** squares and 8-1/2-inch **ORANGE #2** square.

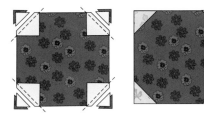

Make 1 Orange #1
Make 1 Orange #2

Step 2   Position a 2-1/2-inch **GREEN #1** square on the right corner of a 2-1/2 x 5-1/2-inch **BEIGE** rectangle. Draw diagonal line on square; stitch on line, trim, and press. Sew a 2-1/2 x 3-1/2-inch **BEIGE** rectangle to right edge of unit; press.

Make 2

Step 3   Sew Step 2 stem units to top edge of Step 1 pumpkin units; press. <u>At this point each pumpkin block should measure 8-1/2 x 10-1/2-inches.</u>

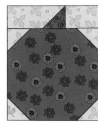

Make 1, Orange #1
Make 1, Orange #2

Step 4   Sew together pumpkin blocks and 2-1/2 x 10-1/2-inch **BEIGE** rectangles; press. <u>At this point the pumpkin section should measure 10-1/2 x 22-1/2-inches.</u>

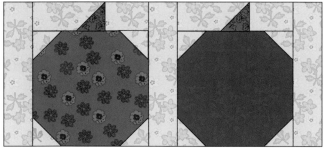

Make 1 Pumpkin Section

Maple Leaf Block
Block Two

Make 6 blocks

Piecing

Note: *Instructions direct you to make one leaf block using* **GREEN #1** *fabric. Repeat the steps to make remaining leaf blocks.*

Step 1   With right sides together, layer 2-7/8-inch **GREEN #1** square and 2-7/8-inch **BEIGE** square. Press together, but do not sew. Cut layered square in half diagonally to make 2 sets of triangles. Stitch 1/4-inch from diagonal edge of each triangle set; press. Sew the triangle-pieced squares together. Sew 2-1/2-inch **GREEN #1** square to left edge of the unit; press. <u>At this point the unit should</u>

Make 2, 2-1/2-inch triangle-pieced squares   *Make 1*

<u>measure 2-1/2 x 6-1/2-inches.</u>

Step 2   Position a 2-1/2-inch **BEIGE** square on the left corner of a 2-1/2 x 6-1/2-inch **GREEN #1** rectangle. Draw diagonal line on square; stitch

   *Make 1*

on line, trim, and press.

Step 3   Position a 2-1/2-inch **BEIGE** square on the left corner of a 2-1/2 x 4-1/2-inch

       Make 1

GREEN #1 rectangle. Draw diagonal line on square; stitch on line, trim, and press.

Step 4   To make stem unit, center a **BEIGE** triangle on 1 x 5-inch **GREEN #1** rectangle and stitch a 1/4-inch seam. Center another **BEIGE** triangle on opposite edge of **GREEN #1** rectangle; stitch. Press seam allowances toward **GREEN #1** rectangle. Trim stem unit so it measures 2-1/2-inches

Trim ends

Make 1 stem set   *Make 1*

square. Sew stem unit to right edge of Step 3 unit; press. <u>At this point the unit should measure 2-1/2 x 6-1/2-inches.</u>

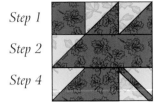

Step 1

Step 2   *Make 1 Green #1*

Step 4

Step 5   Lay out Step 1, Step 2, and Step 4 units, sew together, and press. <u>At this point the leaf block should measure 6-1/2inches square.</u>

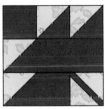   

Make 1 Green #2   *Make 1 Green #3*

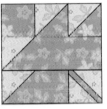   

Make 1 Gold Floral   *Make 2 Rust*

Step 6   Using remaining **GREEN #2**, **GREEN #3**, **GOLD FLORAL**, and **RUST** fabrics, repeat Steps 1 through 5 to make additional leaf blocks.

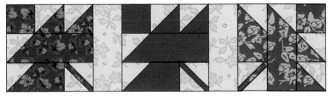

Make 2 Maple Leaf Sections

Step 7   Sew together 3 leaf blocks and 2 of the 2-1/2 x 6-1/2-inch **BEIGE** rectangles; press. Repeat to make another leaf section. <u>At this point each maple leaf section should measure 6-1/2 x 22-1/2-inches.</u>

Step 8 Referring to quilt diagram on page 57, sew maple leaf sections to top and bottom edges of the pumpkin section; press. <u>At this point the pumpkin/leaf section should measure 22-1/2-inches square.</u>

Oak Leaf Section, Quilt Center, & Borders

Note: *Yardage given allows for border strips to be cut on crosswise grain. Diagonally piece strips as needed, referring to* **Diagonal Piecing** *instructions on page 154. Read through* **Borders** *for general instructions on adding borders.*

Cutting

From **RUST PRINT**:
• Cut 2, 2-1/2 x 44-inch strips. From strips cut:
4, 2-1/2 x 8-1/2-inch rectangles
2, 2-1/2 x 4-1/2-inch rectangles
4, 2-1/2-inch squares

From **GOLD FLORAL**:
• Cut 1, 2-1/2 x 44-inch strip. From strip cut:
2, 2-1/2 x 8-1/2-inch rectangles
1, 2-1/2 x 4-1/2-inch rectangle
2, 2-1/2-inch squares

From **BEIGE PRINT**:
• Cut 3, 2-1/2 x 44-inch strips. From strips cut:
9, 2-1/2 x 4-1/2-inch rectangles
18, 2-1/2-inch squares

From **BLACK PRINT**:
• Cut 1, 2-1/2 x 26-1/2-inch strip
• Cut 8, 1-1/2 x 44-inch strips. From strips cut:
2, 1-1/2 x 8-1/2-inch rectangles. Remaining strips will be used for inner and middle border strips.

From **GOLD PRINT**:
• Cut 4, 1-1/2 x 44-inch inner border strips

Oak Leaf Block
Block Two

Make 3 blocks

Piecing

Note: *The instructions direct you to make one leaf block using the* **GOLD FLORAL** *fabric. Repeat the steps to make remaining leaf blocks.*

Step 1 With right sides together, position a 2-1/2-inch **GOLD FLORAL** square on the corner of a 2-1/2 x 4-1/2-inch **BEIGE** rectangle. Draw diagonal line on square; stitch on the line, trim, and press. Repeat this process at opposite corner of rectangle. Sew 2-1/2-inch **BEIGE** squares to both ends of unit; press. <u>At this point the unit should measure 2-1/2 x 8-1/2-inches.</u>

Make 1

Step 2 With right sides together, position 2-1/2-inch **BEIGE** squares on both corners of a 2-1/2 x 8-1/2-inch **GOLD FLORAL** rectangle. Draw diagonal lines on squares; stitch on lines, trim, and press.

Make 2

Step 3 With right sides together, position a 2-1/2 x 4-1/2-inch **BEIGE** rectangle on

the corner of a 2-1/2 x 4-1/2-inch **GOLD FLORAL** rectangle. Draw diagonal line on **BEIGE** rectangle; stitch on line, trim, and press. Repeat this process at opposite corner of **GOLD FLORAL** rectangle.

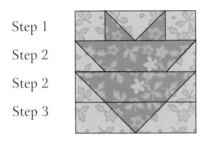

Make 1

Step 4   Lay out Step 1, Step 2, and Step 3 units, sew together, and press. <u>At this point the leaf block should measure 8-1/2-inches square.</u>

Step 1

Step 2

Step 2

Step 3

Make 1 Gold Floral

Step 5   Using **RUST** and **BEIGE** fabrics, repeat Steps 1 through 4 to make additional leaf blocks.

Make 2 Rust

Step 6   Sew together leaf blocks and 1-1/2 x 8-1/2-inch **BLACK** rectangles; press. Sew 2-1/2 x 26-1/2-inch **BLACK** strip to top edge of leaf unit; press. <u>At this point the oak leaf section should measure 10-1/2 x 26-1/2-inches.</u>

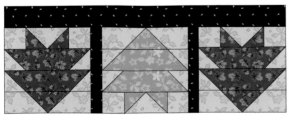

Make 1 Oak Leaf Section

Borders & Quilt Center Assembly

*Note: Yardage given allows for border strips to be cut on crosswise grain. Diagonally piece strips as needed, referring to **Diagonal Piecing** instructions on page 154. Read through **Borders** on page 153 for general instructions on adding borders.*

Attaching Borders

Step 1   Attach 1-1/2-inch wide **BLACK** inner border strips to pumpkin/leaf quilt center.

Step 2   Attach 1-1/2-inch wide **GOLD PRINT** second inner border strips. <u>At this point the quilt center should measure 26-1/2-inches square.</u>

Step 3   Sew oak leaf section (Step 6) to bottom edge of quilt center; press.

Step 4   Attach 1-1/2-inch wide **BLACK** middle border strips. <u>At this point the quilt center should measure 28-1/2 x 38-1/2-inches.</u>

Quilt Center & Border Assembly Diagram

Borders
Outer & Sawtooth Border

Note: *Yardage given allows for border strips to be cut on crosswise grain. Diagonally piece strips as needed. Read through* **Borders** *on page 153 for general instructions on adding borders.*

Cutting

From **BLACK PRINT:**
- Cut 4, 2-7/8 x 44-inch strips

From **RUST/GREEN PRINT:**
- Cut 4, 2-7/8 x 44-inch strips
- Cut 5, 5-1/2 x 44-inch outer border strips

Assemble and Attach Borders

Step 1   Attach 5-1/2-inch wide **RUST/GREEN PRINT** outer border strips.

Step 2   With right sides together, layer 2-7/8 x 44-inch **BLACK** and **RUST/GREEN PRINT** strips together in pairs. Press together, but do not sew. Cut layered strips into squares. Cut layered squares in half diagonally to make 90 sets of triangles. Stitch 1/4-inch from diagonal edge of each set of triangles; press.

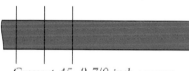

Crosscut 45, 2-7/8-inch squares

Make 90,
2-1/2-inch triangle-pieced squares

Step 3   For side sawtooth borders, sew together 24 triangle-pieced squares; press. Make 2 border strips. Sew sawtooth borders to side edges of quilt center; press. For top/bottom sawtooth borders, sew together 21 triangle-pieced squares; press. Make 2 border strips. Sew sawtooth borders to top/bottom edges of quilt center; press.

Note: *To prevent the sawtooth edges from stretching during the quilting process, we suggest stitching a scant 1/4-inch from the edge of the quilt.*

Putting It All Together

Cut 2-2/3 yard length of backing fabric in half crosswise to make 2, 1-1/3 yard lengths. Refer to **Finishing the Quilt** on page 154 for complete instructions.

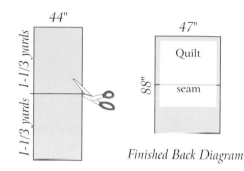

Finished Back Diagram

Quilting Suggestions:

- Pumpkin blocks
  TB60—7-1/2" Snowflake

- All **BEIGE**—stipple

- Maple leaf blocks
  TB52—5-1/2" Oak Leaf

- **BLACK** 1" & **GOLD** 1" borders
  quilt as 1 border
  TB30—1-1/2" Beadwork

- **BLACK** 2" horizontal border
  1" channel stitching

- **BLACK** middle border-in-the-ditch

- Oak leaf blocks—echo

- **RUST/GREEN** outer border/sawtooth—meander

Thimbleberries® *quilt stencils by Quilting Creations International are available at your local quilt shop or visit www.quiltingcreations.com.*

Binding

Note: Because of the outer sawtooth border points, sew binding to quilt using a <u>1/4-inch seam allowance</u> so the tips won't be cut off.

Cutting

From **BLACK PRINT**:
• Cut 5, 2-1/2 x 44-inch strips

Sew binding to quilt using 1/4-inch seam allowance. This measurement will produce a 3/8-inch wide finished double binding. Refer to **Binding** and **Diagonal Piecing** on page 154 for complete instructions.

Autumn Glow Wall Quilt
42 x 52-inches

WINTER DAZZLE THROW

56-inches square

Fabrics & Supplies

3/8 yard **RED PRINT #1** for flower blocks

1/4 yard **GOLD PRINT #1** for flower centers

1/2 yard **GREEN PRINT #1**
for flower blocks, nine-patch blocks

1/4 yard **GREEN PRINT #2** for flower blocks

3/4 yard **BEIGE PRINT** for background

1/3 yard **GOLD PRINT #2**
for nine-patch blocks, corner squares

1/3 yard **BLACK PRINT** for inner border

1 yard **GREEN PRINT #3**
for pieced border, outer border

2/3 yard **RED PRINT #2** for pieced border

1/2 yard **RED PRINT #1** for binding

3-1/2 yards for backing

quilt batting, at least 62-inches square

*Before beginning this project,
read through* **Getting Started** *on page 145.*

Winter Dazzle Throw
Flower Block

Make 5 blocks

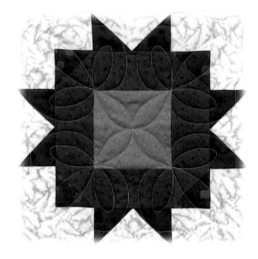

Cutting

From **RED PRINT #1**:
- Cut 3, 2-1/2 x 44-inch strips. From strips cut:
  10, 2-1/2 x 8-1/2-inch rectangles
- Cut 2 more 2-1/2 x 44-inch strips

From **GOLD PRINT #1**:
- Cut 1, 4-1/2 x 44-inch strip

From **GREEN PRINT #1**:
- Cut 2, 2-1/2 x 44-inch strips. From strips cut:
  20, 2-1/2-inch squares

From **GREEN PRINT #2**:
- Cut 3, 2-1/2 x 44-inch strips. From strips cut:
  40, 2-1/2-inch squares

From **BEIGE PRINT**:
- Cut 6, 2-1/2 x 44-inch strips. From strips cut:
  40, 2-1/2 x 4-1/2-inch rectangles
  20, 2-1/2-inch squares

Piecing

Step 1 Aligning long edges, sew 2-1/2 x 44-inch **RED #1** strips to both side edges of a 4-1/2 x 44-inch **GOLD #1** strip; press. Cut strip set into segments.

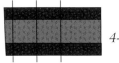

Crosscut 5, 4-1/2-inch wide segments

Step 2 With right sides together, position 2-1/2-inch **GREEN #1** squares on both corners of a 2-1/2 x 8-1/2-inch **RED #1** rectangle. Draw diagonal line on **GREEN #1** squares; stitch on lines. Trim seam allowances to 1/4-inch; press. At this point each unit should measure 2-1/2 x 8-1/2-inches. Sew the units to both side edges of the Step 1 segments; press. At this point each unit should measure 8-1/2-inches square.

Make 10

Make 5

Step 3 With right sides together, position a 2-1/2-inch **GREEN #2** square on the corner of a 2-1/2 x 4-1/2-inch **BEIGE** rectangle. Draw diagonal line on **GREEN #2** square; stitch on line, trim, and press. Repeat this process at opposite corner of rectangle. At this point each unit should measure 2-1/2 x 4-1/2-inches.

Make 20

Step 4 Referring to the diagrams for placement, sew 2-1/2-inch **BEIGE** squares to both side edges of 10 of the Step 3 units to make A Units; press. Sew 2-1/2 x 4-1/2-inch **BEIGE** rectangles to both side edges of the 10 remaining Step 3 units to make B Units; press. At this point the A Units should measure 2-1/2 x 8-1/2-inches and B Units should measure 2-1/2 x 12-1/2-inches.

Make 10 Unit A   *Make 10 Unit B*

Step 5 Sew A Units to top and bottom edges of the Step 2 units; press. Sew B Units to side edges of the units; press. At this point each flower block should measure 12-1/2-inches square.

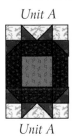

Unit A

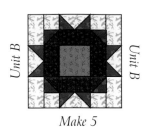

Unit B   *Unit B*

Unit A   *Make 5*

Nine-Patch Blocks, Quilt Center, and Inner Border

Make 4 blocks

Cutting

From **GOLD PRINT #2**:
  • Cut 2, 4-1/2 x 20-inch strips

From **BEIGE PRINT**:
  • Cut 4, 4-1/2 x 20-inch strips

From **GREEN PRINT #1**:
  • Cut 3, 4-1/2 x 20-inch strips

From **BLACK PRINT**:
  • Cut 4, 2-1/2 x 44-inch inner border strips

Piecing

Step 1 Aligning long edges, sew 4-1/2 x 20-inch **GOLD #2** strips to both side edges of a 4-1/2 x 20-inch **BEIGE** strip to make Strip Set A; press. Cut strip set into segments.

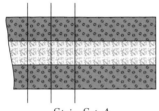

Strip Set A
Crosscut 4, 4-1/2-inch wide segments

Step 2 Aligning long edges, sew 4-1/2 x 20-inch **GREEN #1** strips to both side edges of a 4-1/2 x 20-inch **BEIGE** strip to make Strip Set B; press. Cut strip set into segments.

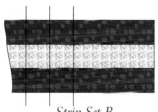

Strip Set B
Crosscut 4, 4-1/2-inch wide segments

Step 3 Aligning long edges, sew 4-1/2 x 20-inch **BEIGE** strips to both side edges of a 4-1/2 x 20-inch **GREEN #1** strip to make Strip Set C; press. Cut strip set into segments.

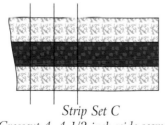

Strip Set C
Crosscut 4, 4-1/2-inch wide segments

Step 4 Referring to diagram, sew Strip Set A, B, and C segments together to make a nine-patch block; press. At this point each nine-patch block should measure 12-1/2-inches square.

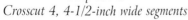

Strip Set A
Strip Set C   *Make 4*
Strip Set B

Step 5 Referring to quilt center assembly diagram, sew flower blocks and nine-patch blocks together in 3 horizontal rows. Press seam allowances in alternating directions by rows so seams will fit snugly together with less bulk. Sew rows together; press.

Step 6 To attach 2-1/2-inch wide **BLACK** inner border strips, refer to *Border* instructions on page 153. At this point the quilt center should measure 40-1/2-inches square.

Quilt Center Assembly Diagram

Borders

*Note: Yardage given allows for borders to be cut on crosswise grain. Diagonally piece strips together as needed. Refer to **Diagonal Piecing** on page 154 for complete instructions. Read through **Border** instructions on page 153 for general instructions on adding borders.*

Cutting

From **GREEN PRINT #3**:
- Cut 6, 4-1/2 x 44-inch outer border strips
- Cut 3, 2-1/2 x 44-inch strips. From strips cut: 40, 2-1/2-inch squares

From **RED PRINT #2**:
- Cut 5, 4-1/2 x 44-inch strips. From strips cut: 20, 4-1/2 x 8-1/2-inch rectangles

From **GOLD PRINT #2**:
- Cut 1, 4-1/2 x 20-1/2-inch strip. From strip cut: 4, 4-1/2-inch corner squares

Piecing

Step 1 With right sides together, position 2-1/2-inch **GREEN #3** squares on both upper corners of a 4-1/2 x 8-1/2-inch **RED #2** rectangle. Draw diagonal line on **GREEN #3** squares; stitch on lines, trim, and press. <u>At this point each unit should measure 4-1/2 x 8-1/2-inches.</u>

Make 20

Step 2 Sew 5 of the Step 1 units together; press. Make 4 pieced border strips. <u>At this point each border strip should measure 4-1/2 x 40-1/2-inches.</u> Sew 2 of the pieced border strips to top and bottom edges of quilt center; press.

Make 4

Step 3 Sew 4-1/2-inch **GOLD #2** corner squares to both ends of remaining pieced border strips; press. Sew the border strips to sides of quilt center; press.

Step 4 Attach 4-1/2-inch wide **GREEN #3** outer border strips.

Putting It All Together

• Cut 3-1/2 yard length of backing fabric in half crosswise to make 2, 1-3/4 yard lengths. Refer to *Finishing the Quilt* on page 154 for complete instructions.

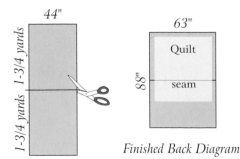

Finished Back Diagram

Quilting Suggestions:

• Flower blocks
   TB8—11" Leaf Quartet

• Nine-Patch blocks-big X in each square

• **BLACK** border
   TB67—1-1/2" Heart Chain

• **RED** border
   channel stitch 2" apart

• **GOLD** corner squares
   TB56—3-1/2" Ice Crystal

• **GREEN** outer border & triangles
   meander

Thimbleberries® *quilt stencils by Quilting Creations International are available at your local quilt shop or visit www.quiltingcreations.com.*

Binding

Cutting

From **RED PRINT #1**:
   • Cut 6, 2-3/4 x 44-inch strips

Sew binding to quilt using 3/8-inch seam allowance. This measurement will produce a 1/2-inch wide finished double binding. Refer to **Binding** and **Diagonal Piecing** on page 154 for complete instructions.

Winter Dazzle Throw
56-inches square

Crazy Quilt Puzzle Quilt

*C*reate an inventive and inviting 12-block masterpiece
of traditional ingenuity with an adventure in crazy quilting.

Leave it to Thimbleberries® Lynette Jensen to show how to
easily bring together simple piecing shapes in a clever and unique
crazy quilt arrangement. Pinwheels, stars, hearts, flying geese,
four patch, rail fence, and hourglass blocks are just a few of the
familiar blocks incorporated into your choice of a delightful spring
option or a rich, traditional holiday quilt or throw.

With Lynette's reliable techniques, you are
going to love the satisfying, successful results.

CRAZY QUILT PUZZLE QUILT

62 x 74-inches
Block size: 12-inches square

Fabrics & Supplies

3/4 yard **LARGE BROWN FLORAL**
for blocks (a bit extra allowed to fussy cut pieces)

2-3/4 yards **ROSE/GOLD FLORAL**
for blocks, outer border (cut lengthwise)

3/8 yard **MEDIUM BROWN FLORAL** for blocks

5/8 yard **TONAL ROSE FLORAL**
for blocks, inner border

1/3 yard **CHESTNUT PRINT** for blocks

3/4 yard **GOLD FLORAL** for blocks, middle border

1/3 yard **LIGHT GREEN PRINT** for blocks

1/4 yard **MEDIUM GREEN PRINT** for blocks

1/3 yard **DARK GREEN PRINT** for blocks

5/8 yard **LIGHT GOLD PRINT**
for blocks, middle border

1/4 yard **DARK BROWN PRINT** for blocks

5/8 yard **BEIGE PRINT** for blocks

2/3 yard **MEDIUM GREEN PRINT** for binding

3-3/4 yards for backing

quilt batting, at least 68 x 82-inches

*Before beginning this project,
read through **Getting Started** on page 145.*

Special Cutting Instructions for **ROSE/GOLD FLORAL**:
• Cut 1, 18 x 44-inch strip. Use this strip to cut the pieces for the Blocks.

*(Set the remaining 2-1/4 yards (81-inch length) aside to be used for the outer border. This yardage will be cut **lengthwise** into 4 outer border strips that are 8-12-inches wide. See page 85 for border cutting instructions.)*

Crazy Quilt Puzzle
Block One

Cutting

From **LARGE BROWN FLORAL**:
• Cut 1, 7-1/2-inch square

From **ROSE/GOLD FLORAL**:
• Cut 1, 2-1/2 x 44-inch strip. From strip cut:
  2, 2-1/2 x 6-1/2-inch rectangles
  2, 2-1/2 x 4-1/2-inch rectangles

From **LIGHT GREEN PRINT**:
• Cut 1, 1 x 44-inch strip. From strip cut:
  2, 1 x 8-1/2-inch rectangles
  2, 1 x 7-1/2-inch rectangles

From **DARK GREEN PRINT**:
• Cut 2, 2-7/8-inch squares

From **CHESTNUT PRINT**:
• Cut 4, 2-7/8-inch squares

From **BEIGE PRINT**:
• Cut 6, 2-7/8-inch squares

Piecing

Step 1   Sew 1 x 7-1/2-inch **LIGHT GREEN** rectangles to top/bottom edges of 7-1/2-inch **LARGE BROWN FLORAL** square; press. Sew 1 x 8-1/2-inch **LIGHT GREEN** rectangles to side edges of center square; press. <u>At this point center unit should measure 8-1/2-inches square.</u>

Make 1

Step 2   With right sides together, layer the 2-7/8-inch **DARK GREEN** squares and 2 of the 2-7/8-inch **BEIGE** squares together in pairs. Press together, but do not sew. Cut layered squares in half diagonally to make 3 triangle sets (you will have 1 extra set). Stitch 1/4-inch from diagonal edge of each triangle set; press.

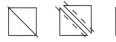

Make 3, 2-1/2-inch triangle-pieced squares

Step 3   With right sides together, layer the 2-7/8-inch **CHESTNUT** squares and 4 of the 2-7/8-inch **BEIGE** squares together in pairs. Press together, but do not sew. Cut layered squares in half diagonally to make 7 triangle sets (you will have 1 extra set). Stitch 1/4-inch from diagonal edge of each triangle set; press.

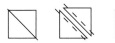

Make 7, 2-1/2-inch triangle-pieced squares

Step 4   Sew a Step 2 **GREEN** triangle-pieced square to left edge of a 2-1/2 x 4-1/2-inch **ROSE/GOLD FLORAL** rectangle. Sew a Step 3 **CHESTNUT** triangle-pieced square to right edge; press. Sew unit to top edge of Step 1 unit; press. <u>At this point center unit should measure 8-1/2 x 10-1/2-inches.</u>

Make 1

Step 5   Sew a Step 3 **CHESTNUT** triangle-pieced square to left edge of a 2-1/2 x 6-1/2-inch **ROSE/GOLD FLORAL** rectangle; press. Sew unit to bottom edge of Step 4 unit; press. <u>At this point center unit should measure 8-1/2 x 12-1/2-inches.</u>

Make 1

Make 1

Step 6   Sew 2 of the Step 2 **GREEN** triangle-pieced squares to top edge of a 2-1/2 x 4-1/2-inch **ROSE/GOLD FLORAL** rectangle. Sew 2 of the Step 3 **CHESTNUT** triangle-pieced squares to bottom edge of unit; press. Sew unit to left edge of center unit; press. <u>At this point center unit should measure 10-1/2 x 12-1/2-inches.</u>

Make 1   *Make 1*

Step 7   Sew 2 of the Step 3 **CHESTNUT** triangle-pieced squares to top edge of a 2-1/2 x 6-1/2-inch **ROSE/GOLD FLORAL** rectangle. Sew 1 of the **CHESTNUT** triangle-pieced squares to bottom edge of unit; press. Sew unit to right edge of center unit; press. <u>At this point the block should measure 12-1/2-inches square.</u>

Make 1   *Make 1*

Block 1

Crazy Quilt Puzzle
Block Two

Cutting

From **LARGE BROWN FLORAL**:
- Cut 1, 4 x 7-1/2-inch rectangle

From **ROSE/GOLD FLORAL**:
- Cut 1, 3-1/2 x 7-1/2-inch rectangle

From **MEDIUM BROWN FLORAL**:
- Cut 1, 3-1/2 x 22-inch strip. From strip cut:
  1, 3-1/2 x 4-inch rectangle
  1, 2-7/8-inch square
  2, 2-1/2 x 4-1/2-inch rectangles
  1, 2-1/2-inch square

From **LIGHT GOLD PRINT**:
- Cut 1, 2-7/8 x 22-inch strip. From strip cut:
  1, 2-7/8-inch square
  2, 2-1/2 x 4-1/2-inch rectangles
  2, 2-1/2-inch squares

From **BEIGE PRINT**:
- Cut 1, 2-7/8-inch square
- Cut 2, 2-1/2-inch squares

From **CHESTNUT PRINT**:
- Cut 1, 2-7/8 x 22-inch strip. From strip cut:
  1, 2-7/8-inch square
  1, 2-1/2 x 4-1/2-inch rectangle
  1, 1-1/2 x 12-1/2-inch rectangle

From **MEDIUM GREEN PRINT**:
- Cut 1, 2-1/2 x 5-1/2-inch rectangle

From **GOLD FLORAL**:
- Cut 1, 4 x 4-1/2-inch rectangle

Piecing

Step 1 With right sides together, position a 2-1/2-inch **LIGHT GOLD** square on the right corner of a 2-1/2 x 4-1/2-inch **MEDIUM BROWN FLORAL** rectangle. Draw diagonal line on square and stitch on line. Trim seam allowance to 1/4-inch; press.

Make 2

Step 2 With right sides together, position a 2-1/2-inch **MEDIUM BROWN FLORAL** square on the left corner of a 2-1/2 x 4-1/2-inch **LIGHT GOLD** rectangle. Draw diagonal line on square; stitch on line, trim, and press.

Make 1

Step 3 Repeat Step 2 using a 2-1/2-inch **BEIGE** square and a 2-1/2 x 4-1/2-inch **LIGHT GOLD** rectangle.

Make 1

Step 4 With right sides together, layer the 2-7/8-inch **LIGHT GOLD** and **MEDIUM BROWN FLORAL** squares. Press together, but do not sew. Cut layered square in half diagonally to make 1 triangle set (you will have 1 extra set). Stitch 1/4-inch from diagonal edge of triangle set; press. Repeat this step using the 2-7/8-inch **CHESTNUT** and **BEIGE** squares.

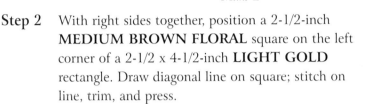

Make 1, 2-1/2-inch triangle-pieced square

Make 1, 2-1/2-inch triangle-pieced square

Step 5 Referring to diagram for placement, sew 2-1/2 x 4-1/2-inch **CHESTNUT** rectangle to top edge of a Step 1 unit; press. Sew 2-1/2-inch **BEIGE** square to left edge of Step 4 **LIGHT GOLD/MEDIUM BROWN FLORAL** triangle-pieced square; press. Sew unit to bottom edge of Step 2 unit; press. Sew a Step 1 unit to top edge of Step 3 unit; press. Sew units together; press. <u>At this point the unit should measure 4-1/2 x 12-1/2-inches.</u>

Step 1

Step 2
Step 4

Step 1
Step 3

Make 1

Step 6 Referring to diagram, sew together the 4 x 4-1/2-inch **GOLD FLORAL** rectangle and 3-1/2 x 4-inch **MEDIUM BROWN FLORAL** rectangle; press. Sew the 4 x 7-1/2-inch **LARGE BROWN FLORAL** rectangle to top edge of unit. Sew the Step 4 **CHESTNUT/ BEIGE** triangle-pieced square to left edge of the 2-1/2 x 5-1/2-inch **MEDIUM GREEN** rectangle; press. Sew 3-1/2 x 7-1/2-inch **ROSE/GOLD FLORAL** rectangle to top edge of unit; press. Sew units together; press. <u>At this point the unit should measure 7-1/2 x 12-1/2-inches.</u>

Make 1

Step 7 Sew Step 5 and Step 6 units to both side edges of the 1-1/2 x 12-1/2-inch **CHESTNUT** rectangle; press. <u>At this point the block should measure 12-1/2-inches square.</u>

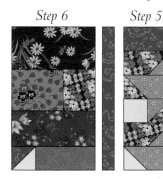

Step 6   *Step 5*

Make 1
Block 2

Crazy Quilt Puzzle
Block Three

Cutting

From **LARGE BROWN FLORAL**:
• Cut 2, 4-inch squares

From **ROSE/GOLD FLORAL**:
• Cut 1, 3-1/2 x 8-1/2-inch rectangle

From **MEDIUM BROWN FLORAL**:
• Cut 2, 2-1/2 x 6-1/2-inch rectangles

From **LIGHT GOLD PRINT**:
• Cut 1, 4-inch square
• Cut 2, 2-1/2-inch squares

From **DARK BROWN PRINT**:
• Cut 1, 4-inch square

From **LIGHT GREEN PRINT**:
• Cut 5, 2-1/2-inch squares
• Cut 1, 1-1/2 x 7-1/2-inch rectangle

From **GOLD FLORAL**:
• Cut 5, 2-1/2-inch squares

Piecing

Step 1 With right sides together, position a 2-1/2-inch **LIGHT GOLD** square on right corner of each 2-1/2 x 6-1/2-inch **MEDIUM BROWN FLORAL** rectangle. Draw diagonal line on each square; stitch on line, trim, and press. Sew units together; press. At this point the unit should measure 2-1/2 x 12-1/2-inches.

Make 2

Make 1

Step 2 Sew together 3 of the 2 1/2 inch **GOLD FLORAL** squares and 3 of the 2-1/2-inch **LIGHT GREEN** squares; press. At this point the unit should measure 2-1/2 x 12-1/2-inches.

Make 1

Step 3 Sew together 2 of the 2-1/2-inch **GOLD FLORAL** squares and 2 of the 2-1/2-inch **LIGHT GREEN** squares; press. Sew the unit to bottom edge of the 3-1/2 x 8-1/2-inch **ROSE/GOLD FLORAL** rectangle. At this point the unit should measure 5-1/2 x 8-1/2-inches.

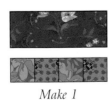

Make 1

Step 4 Sew the 4-inch **LARGE BROWN FLORAL** squares to the 4-inch **DARK BROWN** square and the 4-inch **LIGHT GOLD** square; press.

Sew both units to the side edges of the 1-1/2 x 7-1/2-inch **LIGHT GREEN** rectangle. At this point the unit should measure 7-1/2 x 8-1/2-inches.

Make 1

Step 5 Sew Step 4 unit to top edge of Step 3 unit; press. At this point the unit should measure 8-1/2 x 12-1/2-inches.

Step 4

Step 3

Make 1

Step 6 Sew Step 1 and Step 2 units to both side edges of Step 5 unit; press. At this point the block should measure 12-1/2-inches square.

Step 1

Step 2

Make 1
Block 3

Crazy Quilt Puzzle
Block Four

Cutting

From LARGE BROWN FLORAL:
• Cut 2, 4-inch squares

From ROSE/GOLD FLORAL:
• Cut 1, 4-1/2 x 6-1/2-inch rectangle

From LIGHT GOLD PRINT:
• Cut 4, 2-1/2-inch squares

From BEIGE PRINT:
• Cut 1, 2-7/8 x 44-inch strip. From strip cut:
  1, 2-7/8-inch square
  1, 2-1/2 x 6-1/2-inch rectangle
  1, 2-1/2 x 4-1/2-inch rectangle
  1, 1-1/2 x 8-1/2-inch rectangle
  1, 1-1/2 x 7-1/2-inch rectangle

From CHESTNUT PRINT:
• Cut 1, 2-7/8-inch square

From MEDIUM BROWN FLORAL:
• Cut 1, 4-1/2-inch square

From MEDIUM GREEN PRINT:
• Cut 1, 2-1/2 x 8-1/2-inch rectangle

From DARK BROWN PRINT:
• Cut 1, 4-inch square

From DARK GREEN PRINT:
• Cut 1, 4-inch square

Step 1 With right sides together, position a 2-1/2-inch **LIGHT GOLD** square on the corner of a 2-1/2 x 4-1/2-inch **BEIGE** rectangle. Draw diagonal line on square; stitch on line, trim, and press. Repeat this process at opposite corner of rectangle. Sew unit to right edge of 4-1/2 x 6-1/2-inch **ROSE/GOLD FLORAL** rectangle. <u>At this point the unit should measure 4-1/2 x 8-1/2-inches</u>.

Make 1

Make 1

Step 2 Sew the 4-inch **LARGE BROWN FLORAL** squares to the 4-inch **DARK GREEN** square and the 4-inch **DARK BROWN** square; press. Sew units together; press. Sew a 1-1/2 x 7-1/2-inch **BEIGE** rectangle to bottom edge of square and sew a 1-1/2 x 8-1/2-inch **BEIGE** rectangle to right edge; press. <u>At this point the unit should measure 8-1/2-inches square</u>.

Make 1

Step 3 Sew Step 1 unit to bottom edge of Step 2 unit; press. <u>At this point the unit should measure 8-1/2 x 12-1/2-inches</u>.

Make 1

Step 4 With right sides together, position a 2-1/2-inch **LIGHT GOLD** square on the right corner of the 2-1/2 x 8-1/2-inch **MEDIUM GREEN** rectangle. Draw diagonal line on square; stitch on line, trim, and press.

Make 1

Step 5 With right sides together, position a 2-1/2-inch **LIGHT GOLD** square on the right corner of the 2-1/2 x 6-1/2-inch **BEIGE** rectangle. Draw diagonal line on square; stitch on line, trim, and press.

Make 1

Step 6 With right sides together, layer the 2-7/8-inch **BEIGE** and **CHESTNUT** squares together. Press together, but do not sew. Cut layered square in half diagonally to make 1 set of triangles (you will have 1 extra set). Stitch 1/4-inch from diagonal edge of the triangle set; press. Sew triangle-pieced square to left edge of Step 5 unit; press.

 Step 5

Make 1, 2-1/2-inch triangle-pieced square　　*Make 1*

Step 7 Sew together Step 4 and Step 6 units; press. Sew the 4-1/2-inch **MEDIUM BROWN FLORAL** square to unit; press. <u>At this point the unit should measure 4-1/2 x 12-1/2-inches.</u>

Step 4　　*Step 6*

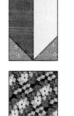

Make 1

Step 8 Sew together Step 3 and Step 7 units; press. <u>At this point the block should measure 12-1/2-inches square.</u>

Step 3　　*Step 7*

Make 1 Block 4

Crazy Quilt Puzzle
Block Five

Cutting

From LARGE BROWN FLORAL:
- Cut 1, 4 x 7-1/2-inch rectangle

From ROSE/GOLD FLORAL:
- Cut 1, 3 x 7-1/2 inch rectangle

From CHESTNUT PRINT:
- Cut 1, 2-7/8-inch square
- Cut 5, 2-1/2 x 4-1/2-inch rectangles

From BEIGE PRINT:
- Cut 1, 2-7/8 x 44-inch strip. From strip cut 1, 2-7/8-inch square 10, 2-1/2-inch squares

From MEDIUM BROWN FLORAL:
- Cut 1, 2-7/8-inch square
- Cut 1, 2-1/2-inch square

From LIGHT GOLD PRINT:
- Cut 1, 2-7/8-inch square
- Cut 2, 2-1/2-inch squares

From TONAL ROSE FLORAL:
- Cut 1, 2-1/2 x 6-1/2-inch rectangle
- Cut 1, 2-1/2 x 4-1/2-inch rectangle

From LIGHT GREEN PRINT:
- Cut 1, 3-1/2 x 6-1/2-inch rectangle

From DARK BROWN PRINT:
- Cut 1, 2-1/2 x 6-1/2-inch rectangle

73

Piecing

Step 1 With right sides together, position a 2-1/2-inch **BEIGE** square on the corner of a 2-1/2 x 4-1/2-inch **CHESTNUT** rectangle. Draw diagonal line on square; stitch on line, trim, and press. Repeat this process at opposite corner of rectangle. Make 5 flying geese units. Sew units together; press. <u>At this point the flying geese unit should measure 4-1/2 x 10-1/2-inches.</u>

Make 5
flying geese units   *Make 1*

Step 2 With right sides together, layer the 2-7/8-inch **LIGHT GOLD** and **MEDIUM BROWN FLORAL** squares. Press together, but do not sew. Cut layered square in half diagonally to make 1 set of triangles (you will have 1 extra set). Stitch 1/4-inch from diagonal edge of triangle set; press. Sew triangle-pieced square to right edge of 2-1/2-inch **MEDIUM BROWN FLORAL** square; press. Sew unit to top edge of Step 1 flying geese unit; press. <u>At this point the unit should measure 4-1/2 x 12-1/2-inches.</u>

Make 1,   *Make 1*   *Make 1*
2-1/2-inch
triangle-pieced square

Step 3 Sew 4 x 7-1/2-inch **LARGE BROWN FLORAL** rectangle to left edge of 3 x 7-1/2-inch **ROSE/GOLD FLORAL** rectangle; press. Sew 2-1/2 x 6-1/2-inch **DARK BROWN** rectangle to top edge of unit and sew 3-1/2 x 6-1/2-inch **LIGHT GREEN** rectangle to bottom edge of unit; press. <u>At this point the unit should measure 6-1/2 x 12-1/2-inches.</u>

Make 1

Step 4 With right sides together, position a 2-1/2-inch **LIGHT GOLD** square on the corner of a 2-1/2 x 4-1/2-inch **TONAL ROSE FLORAL** rectangle. Draw diagonal line on square; stitch on line, trim, and press. Repeat this process at opposite corner of rectangle. Sew unit to 2-1/2 x 6-1/2-inch **TONAL ROSE FLORAL** rectangle; press. <u>At this point the unit should measure 2-1/2 x 10-1/2-inches.</u>

Make 1   *Make 1*

Step 5 With right sides together, layer the 2-7/8-inch **BEIGE** and **CHESTNUT** squares. Press together, but do not sew. Cut layered square in half diagonally to make 1 set of triangles (you will have 1 extra set). Stitch 1/4-inch from diagonal edge of triangle set; press. Sew triangle-pieced square to top edge of Step 4 unit; press. <u>At this point the unit should measure 2-1/2 x 12-1/2-inches.</u>

Make 1,   *Make 1*
2-1/2-inch
triangle-pieced square

Step 6 Sew together Step 2, Step 3, and Step 5 units; press. <u>At this point the block should measure 12-1/2-inches square.</u>

Step 5   *Step 3*   *Step 2*

Make 1
Block 5

Crazy Quilt Puzzle
Block Six

Cutting

From **LARGE BROWN FLORAL**:
• Cut 1, 7-1/2-inch square

From **ROSE/GOLD FLORAL**:
• Cut 1, 5-1/2 x 12-1/2-inch rectangle

From **DARK GREEN PRINT**:
• Cut 3, 2-1/2 x 4-1/2-inch rectangles

From **BEIGE PRINT**:
• Cut 6, 2-1/2-inch squares

From **CHESTNUT PRINT**:
• Cut 1, 1-1/2 x 6-1/2-inch rectangle

From **MEDIUM GREEN PRINT**:
• Cut 1, 1-1/2 x 5-1/2-inch rectangle

Piecing

Step 1 Position a 2-1/2-inch **BEIGE** square on the corner of a 2-1/2 x 4-1/2-inch **DARK GREEN** rectangle. Draw diagonal line on square; stitch on line, trim, and press. Repeat this process at opposite corner of rectangle. Make 3 flying geese units. Sew units together; press. At this point the flying geese unit should measure 4-1/2 x 6-1/2-inches.

Make 3,
flying geese
units

Make 1

Step 2 Sew 1-1/2 x 6-1/2-inch **CHESTNUT** rectangle to top edge of flying geese unit and sew 1-1/2 x 5-1/2-inch **MEDIUM GREEN** rectangle to right edge of unit; press. At this point the unit should measure 5-1/2 x 7-1/2-inches.

Make 1

Step 1

Step 3 Sew 7-1/2-inch **LARGE BROWN FLORAL** square to top edge of Step 2 unit; press. At this point the unit should measure 7-1/2 x 12-1/2-inches.

Make 1

Step 4 Sew Step 3 unit to right edge of 5-1/2 x 12-1/2-inch **ROSE/GOLD FLORAL** rectangle; press. At this point the block should measure 12-1/2-inches square.

Step 3

Make 1
Block 6

Crazy Quilt Puzzle
Block Seven

Cutting

From **LARGE BROWN FLORAL**:
• Cut 1, 7-1/2-inch square

From **ROSE/GOLD FLORAL**:
• Cut 1, 3-1/2 x 7-1/2-inch rectangle

From **GOLD FLORAL**:
• Cut 4, 2-7/8-inch squares

From **BEIGE PRINT**:
• Cut 4, 2-7/8-inch squares
• Cut 1, 2-1/2 x 4-1/2-inch rectangle

From **LIGHT GOLD PRINT**:
• Cut 2, 2-1/2-inch squares

From **TONAL ROSE FLORAL**:
• Cut 1, 1-1/2 x 10-1/2-inch rectangle

From **LIGHT GREEN PRINT**:
• Cut 1, 2-1/2 x 8-1/2-inch rectangle

From **MEDIUM GREEN PRINT**:
• Cut 2, 2-1/2-inch squares

Piecing

Step 1 With right sides together, layer the 2-7/8-inch **BEIGE** and **GOLD FLORAL** squares in pairs. Press together, but do not sew. Cut layered squares diagonally in half to make 8 sets of triangles. Stitch 1/4-inch from diagonal edge of each set of triangles; press. Sew together 5 triangle-pieced squares; press. Sew a 2-1/2-inch **MEDIUM GREEN** square to right edge of triangle-pieced square unit; press. <u>At this point the unit should measure 2-1/2 x 12-1/2-inches.</u>

Make 8,
2-1/2-inch
triangle-pieced squares

Make 1

Step 2 Sew together 3 triangle-pieced squares; press. Sew a 2-1/2-inch **MEDIUM GREEN** square to bottom edge of triangle-pieced square unit; press.

Make 1

Step 3 Sew together the 7-1/2-inch **LARGE BROWN FLORAL** square and the 3-1/2 x 7-1/2-inch **ROSE/GOLD FLORAL** rectangle; press. Sew 1-1/2 x 10-1/2-inch **TONAL ROSE FLORAL** rectangle to bottom edge of unit; press. Sew Step 2 unit to left edge of unit; press. <u>At this point the unit should measure 8-1/2 x 12-1/2-inches.</u>

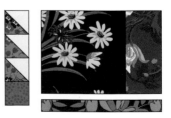

Make 1

Step 4   With right sides together, position a 2-1/2-inch **LIGHT GOLD** square on the corner of a 2-1/2 x 4-1/2-inch **BEIGE** rectangle. Draw diagonal line on square; stitch on line, trim, and press. Repeat this process at opposite corner of rectangle. Sew 2-1/2 x 8-1/2-inch **LIGHT GREEN** rectangle to left edge of unit; press. <u>At this point the unit should measure 2-1/2 x 12-1/2-inches</u>

Make 1

Make 1

Step 5   Sew together Step 1, Step 3, and Step 4 units; press. <u>At this point the block should measure 12-1/2-inches square.</u>

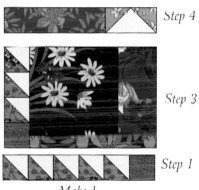

Step 4

Step 3

Step 1

Make 1
Block 7

Crazy Quilt Puzzle
Block Eight

Cutting

From **LARGE BROWN FLORAL**:
• Cut 1, 4 x 7-1/2-inch rectangle

From **ROSE/GOLD FLORAL**:
• Cut 1, 4 x 7-1/2-inch rectangle

From **MEDIUM GREEN PRINT**:
• Cut 1, 3-1/2 x 7-1/2-inch rectangle

From **CHESTNUT PRINT**:
• Cut 1, 3-1/2-inch square

From **BEIGE PRINT**:
• Cut 2, 2-7/8-inch squares
• Cut 4, 1-1/2-inch squares

From **LIGHT GOLD PRINT**:
• Cut 1, 3-1/2-inch square

From **DARK BROWN PRINT**:
• Cut 1, 2-1/2 x 8-1/2-inch rectangle
• Cut 1, 2 x 4-1/2-inch rectangle

From **DARK GREEN PRINT**:
• Cut 1, 2 x 4-1/2-inch rectangle

From **MEDIUM BROWN FLORAL**:
• Cut 1, 2-7/8-inch square
• Cut 1, 2-1/2-inch square

From **GOLD FLORAL**:
• Cut 1, 2-7/8-inch square

From **LIGHT GREEN PRINT**:
• Cut 1, 2-1/2 x 6 1/2-inch rectangle

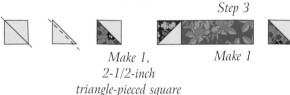

Piecing

Step 1 Sew together 4 x 7-1/2-inch **LARGE BROWN FLORAL** rectangle and 4 x 7-1/2-inch **ROSE/GOLD FLORAL** rectangle; press. Sew 3-1/2 x 7-1/2-inch **MEDIUM GREEN** rectangle to right edge of unit; press. At this point the unit should measure 7-1/2 x 10-1/2-inches.

Make 1

Step 2 With right sides together, position 1-1/2-inch **BEIGE** squares on the corners of 3-1/2-inch **CHESTNUT** square. Draw diagonal line on squares; stitch on lines, trim, and press. Sew 3-1/2-inch **LIGHT GOLD** square to left edge of snowball unit; press. Sew 2 x 4-1/2-inch **DARK BROWN PRINT** and **DARK GREEN** rectangles together; press. Sew unit to right edge of snowball unit; press. At this point the unit should measure 3-1/2 x 10-1/2-inches.

        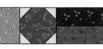

Make 1   *Make 1*

Step 3 With right sides together, layer a 2-7/8-inch **BEIGE** and **MEDIUM BROWN FLORAL** square. Press together, but do not sew. Cut layered square diagonally in half to make 2 sets of triangles. Stitch 1/4-inch from diagonal edge of each set of triangles; press. Sew 1 triangle-pieced square to left edge of 2-1/2 x 6-1/2-inch **LIGHT GREEN** rectangle; press.

Make 2, 2-1/2-inch triangle-pieced squares   *Make 1*

Step 4 Repeat Step 3 using a 2-7/8-inch **BEIGE** and **GOLD FLORAL** square (you will have 1 extra set of triangles) Sew triangle-pieced square to right edge of Step 3 unit; press. At this point the unit should measure 2-1/2 x 10-1/2-inches.

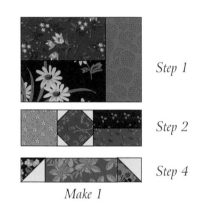

Step 3

Make 1, 2-1/2-inch triangle-pieced square   *Make 1*

Step 5 Sew together Step 1, Step 2, and Step 4 units; press. At this point the unit should measure 10-1/2 x 12-1/2-inches.

Step 1

Step 2

Step 4

Make 1

Step 6 Sew together the 2-1/2 x 8-1/2-inch **DARK BROWN PRINT** rectangle, 1 of the Step 3 triangle-pieced squares, and the 2-1/2-inch **MEDIUM BROWN FLORAL** square; press. Sew unit to left edge of Step 5 unit; press. At this point the block should measure 12-1/2-inches square.

Step 5

Step 3

Make 1
Block 8

Crazy Quilt Puzzle
Block Nine

Cutting

From **LARGE BROWN FLORAL**:
- Cut 2, 4-inch squares

From **ROSE/GOLD FLORAL**:
- Cut 1, 3 x 6 inch rectangle

From **LIGHT GREEN PRINT**:
- Cut 1, 4 x 4-1/2-inch rectangle
- Cut 1, 1 x 4-inch rectangle

From **BEIGE PRINT**:
- Cut 1, 3-inch square
- Cut 1, 2-7/8-inch square
- Cut 1, 1 x 8-inch rectangle
- Cut 4, 1-1/2-inch squares

From **GOLD FLORAL**:
- Cut 3, 4-1/2-inch squares
- Cut 1, 2-7/8-inch square

From **MEDIUM GREEN PRINT**:
- Cut 1, 2-1/2 x 6-inch rectangle
- Cut 1, 2-1/2-inch square

From **DARK BROWN PRINT**:
- Cut 1, 3 x 5-inch rectangle

From **TONAL ROSE FLORAL**:
- Cut 1, 2-1/2-inch square

From **LIGHT GOLD PRINT**:
- Cut 1, 2-1/2-inch square

Piecing

Step 1 Sew 4-inch **LARGE BROWN FLORAL** squares to both side edges of 1 x 4-inch **LIGHT GREEN** rectangle; press. Sew 1 x 8-inch **BEIGE** rectangle to left edge of unit; press. <u>At this point the unit should measure 4-1/2 x 8-inches</u>.

Make 1

Step 2 With right sides together, position 1-1/2-inch **BEIGE** squares on 2 lower corners of the 4-1/2-inch **GOLD FLORAL** squares. Draw diagonal line on squares; stitch on lines, trim, and press. Sew a 4-1/2-inch **GOLD FLORAL** square to top edge of 1 of the units; press.

Make 2   *Make 1*

Step 3 Sew 4 x 4-1/2-inch **LIGHT GREEN** rectangle to bottom edge of remaining Step 2 unit; press. Sew unit to left edge of Step 1 unit; press. <u>At this point the unit should measure 8 x 8-1/2-inches</u>.

Step 2      *Step 1*

Make 1

Step 4 With right sides together, position 3-inch **BEIGE** square on the corner of 3 x 5-inch **DARK BROWN PRINT** rectangle. Draw diagonal line on square; stitch on line, trim, and press. Sew together 3 x 6-inch **ROSE/GOLD FLORAL** rectangle and 2-1/2 x 6-inch **MEDIUM GREEN** rectangle; press. Sew unit to left edge of **BEIGE/BROWN** unit; press. At this point the unit should measure 5 x 8-1/2-inches.

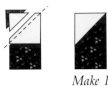

Make 1   *Make 1*

Step 5 Sew together 2-1/2-inch **TONAL ROSE FLORAL** and **LIGHT GOLD** squares; press. With right sides together, layer the 2-7/8-inch **BEIGE** and **GOLD FLORAL** squares. Press together, but do not sew. Cut layered square diagonally in half to make 1 triangle set (you will have 1 extra set). Stitch 1/4-inch from diagonal edge of triangle set; press. Sew triangle-pieced square to left edge of 2-1/2-inch **MEDIUM GREEN** square; press. Sew units together; press. At this point the unit should measure 4-1/2-inches square.

Make 1   *Make 1, 2-1/2-inch triangle-pieced square*   *Make 1*

Step 6 Sew together Step 2 and Step 5 units, and Step 3 and Step 4 units; press. Sew units together; press. At this point the block should measure 12-1/2-inches square.

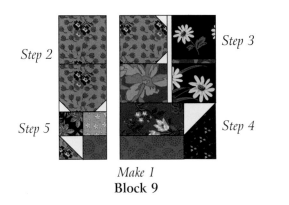

Make 1
Block 9

Crazy Quilt Puzzle
Block Ten

Cutting

From **LARGE BROWN FLORAL**:
• Cut 1, 4 x 7-1/2-inch rectangle

From **ROSE/GOLD FLORAL**:
• Cut 1, 3 x 7-1/2-inch rectangle
• Cut 1, 2-1/2 x 4-1/2-inch rectangle

From **DARK GREEN PRINT**:
• Cut 3, 2-7/8-inch squares

From **BEIGE PRINT**:
• Cut 5, 2-7/8-inch squares
• Cut 3, 2-1/2-inch squares

From **MEDIUM BROWN FLORAL**:
• Cut 1, 2-7/8-inch square
• Cut 1, 2-1/2-inch square

From **GOLD FLORAL**:
• Cut 1, 2-7/8-inch square

From **LIGHT GREEN PRINT**:
• Cut 1, 2-1/2 x 4-1/2-inch rectangle
• Cut 1, 1-1/2 x 5-1/2-inch rectangle

From **DARK BROWN PRINT**:
• Cut 2, 3-inch squares

From **LIGHT GOLD PRINT**:
• Cut 2, 3-inch squares

80

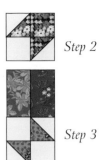

Piecing

Step 1 With right sides together, layer 3 of the 2-7/8-inch **BEIGE** and **DARK GREEN** squares in pairs. Press together, but do not sew. Cut layered squares diagonally in half to make 6 sets of triangles. Stitch 1/4-inch from diagonal edge of each set of triangles; press. Sew triangle-pieced squares together; press. At this point the unit should measure 2-1/2 x 12-1/2-inches.

Make 6, 2-1/2-inch triangle-pieced squares

Make 1

Step 2 Repeat Step 1 using a 2-7/8-inch **MEDIUM BROWN FLORAL** square and a 2-7/8-inch **BEIGE** square. Make 2 triangle-pieced squares. Sew the triangle-pieced squares to a 2-1/2-inch **MEDIUM BROWN FLORAL** square and a 2-1/2-inch **BEIGE** square; press. Sew the units together; press. At this point the unit should measure 4-1/2-inches square.

Make 2, 2-1/2-inch triangle-pieced squares   *Make 1*

Step 3 Repeat Step 1 using a 2-7/8-inch **GOLD FLORAL** square and a 2-7/8-inch **BEIGE** square. Make 2 triangle-pieced squares. Sew the triangle-pieced squares to the 2-1/2-inch **BEIGE** squares; press. Sew the 2 units together; press. At this point the unit should measure 4-1/2-inches square.

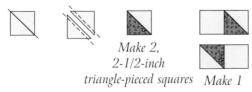

Make 2, 2-1/2-inch triangle-pieced squares   *Make 1*

Step 4 Sew together the 2-1/2 x 4-1/2-inch **LIGHT GREEN** and **ROSE/GOLD FLORAL** rectangles; press. Sew Step 2 unit to top edge of unit and sew Step 3 unit to bottom edge of unit; press. At this point the unit should measure 4-1/2 x 12-1/2-inches.

Step 2

Step 3

Make 1

Step 5 Sew together 3-inch **LIGHT GOLD** and **DARK BROWN** squares; press. Sew 1-1/2 x 5-1/2-inch **LIGHT GREEN** rectangle to left edge of unit; press.

Make 1

Step 6 Sew together 3 x 7-1/2-inch **ROSE/GOLD FLORAL** rectangle and 4 x 7-1/2-inch **LARGE BROWN FLORAL** rectangle; press. Sew Step 5 unit to bottom edge of unit; press. At this point the unit should measure 6-1/2 x 12-1/2-inches.

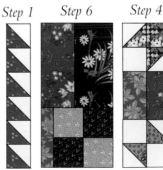

Step 5

Make 1

Step 7 Sew together Step 1, Step 4, and Step 6 units; press. At this point the block should measure 12-1/2-inches square.

Step 1   *Step 6*   *Step 4*

Make 1
Block 10

Crazy Quilt Puzzle
Block Eleven

Cutting

From **LARGE BROWN FLORAL**:
- Cut 2, 4-inch squares

From **ROSE/GOLD FLORAL**:
- Cut 1, 4-1/2-inch square
- Cut 1, 4-inch square
- Cut 1, 2-1/2 x 7-1/2-inch rectangle

From **GOLD FLORAL**:
- Cut 1, 2-7/8-inch square
- Cut 1, 2-1/2-inch square

From **BEIGE PRINT**:
- Cut 1, 2-7/8-inch square

From **TONAL ROSE FLORAL**:
- Cut 1, 2-1/2 x 4-1/2-inch rectangle

From **MEDIUM GREEN PRINT**:
- Cut 2, 2-1/2 x 4-1/2-inch rectangles

From **LIGHT GOLD PRINT**:
- Cut 1, 1-1/2 x 12-1/2-inch rectangle

From **DARK GREEN PRINT**:
- Cut 1, 4-inch square

From **DARK BROWN PRINT**:
- Cut 1, 3-1/2 x 7-1/2-inch rectangle

Piecing

Step 1 With right sides together, layer the 2-7/8-inch **BEIGE** and **GOLD FLORAL** squares. Press together, but do not sew. Cut layered square in half diagonally to make 2 sets of triangles. Stitch 1/4-inch from diagonal edge of each triangle set; press. Sew triangle-pieced squares together; press. Sew 2-1/2 x 4-1/2-inch **TONAL ROSE FLORAL** rectangle to right edge of unit; press. <u>At this point the unit should measure 4-1/2-inches square.</u>

Make 2, 2-1/2-inch triangle-pieced squares   Make 1

Step 2 With right sides together, position 2-1/2-inch **GOLD FLORAL** square on right corner of 2-1/2 x 4-1/2-inch **MEDIUM GREEN** rectangle. Draw diagonal line on square; stitch on line, trim, and press. Sew 4-1/2-inch **ROSE/GOLD FLORAL** square and 2-1/2 x 4-1/2-inch **MEDIUM GREEN** rectangle to bottom edge of unit; press. <u>At this point the unit should measure 4-1/2 x 8-1/2-inches.</u>

Make 1   Make 1

Step 3 Sew Step 1 unit to top edge of Step 2 unit; press. Sew 1-1/2 x 12-1/2-inch **LIGHT GOLD** rectangle to left edge of unit; press. <u>At this point the unit should measure 5-1/2 x 12-1/2-inches.</u>

Step 1

Step 2

Make 1

Step 4 Sew the 4-inch **LARGE BROWN FLORAL** squares to the 4-inch **ROSE/GOLD FLORAL** square and the 4-inch **DARK GREEN** square; press. Sew units together; press. <u>At this point the unit should measure 7-1/2-inches square.</u>

Make 1

Step 5 Sew together 3-1/2 x 7-1/2-inch **DARK BROWN PRINT** rectangle and 2-1/2 x 7-1/2-inch **ROSE/GOLD FLORAL** rectangle; press. Sew Step 4 unit to top edge of unit; press. <u>At this point the unit should measure 7-1/2 x 12-1/2-inches.</u>

Step 4

Make 1

Step 6 Sew together Step 3 and Step 5 units, press. <u>At this point the block should measure 12-1/2-inches square.</u>

Step 5   *Step 3*

Make 1
Block 11

Crazy Quilt Puzzle
Block Twelve

Cutting

From **LARGE BROWN FLORAL**:
- Cut 1, 7-1/2-inch square

From **ROSE/GOLD FLORAL**:
- Cut 1, 2-1/2 x 22-inch strip. From strip cut:
  1, 2-1/2 x 4 1/2-inch rectangle
  1, 1-1/2 x 8-1/2-inch rectangle
  1, 1-1/2 x 7-1/2-inch rectangle

From **GOLD FLORAL**:
- Cut 1, 2-7/8-inch square
- Cut 1, 2-1/2-inch square

From **BEIGE PRINT**:
- Cut 1, 2-7/8-inch square
- Cut 1, 2-1/2 x 4-1/2-inch rectangle

From **TONAL ROSE FLORAL**:
- Cut 1, 2-1/2 x 4-1/2-inch rectangle

From **MEDIUM BROWN FLORAL**:
- Cut 2, 5-1/4-inch squares

From **LIGHT GOLD PRINT**:
- Cut 2, 5-1/4-inch squares

Piecing

Step 1 With right sides together, layer 2-7/8-inch **BEIGE** and **GOLD FLORAL** squares. Press together, but do not sew. Cut layered square in half diagonally to make 2 sets of triangles. Stitch 1/4-inch from diagonal edge of each set of triangles; press. Sew 2-1/2 x 4-1/2-inch **TONAL ROSE FLORAL** rectangle to top edge of 1 triangle-pieced square; press. <u>At this point the unit should measure 2-1/2 x 6-1/2-inches.</u>

 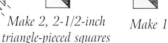 

Make 2, 2-1/2-inch triangle-pieced squares   *Make 1*

Step 2 With right sides together, position 2-1/2-inch **GOLD FLORAL** square on top edge of 2-1/2 x 4-1/2-inch **BEIGE** rectangle. Draw diagonal line on square; stitch on line, trim, and press. Sew 1 triangle-pieced square to top edge of unit; press. Sew Step 1 unit to left edge of unit; press. Sew 2-1/2 x 4-1/2-inch **ROSE/GOLD FLORAL** rectangle to bottom edge of unit; press. <u>At this point the unit should measure 4-1/2 x 8-1/2-inches.</u>

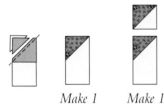

Step 1

Make 1   *Make 1*

Make 1

Step 3 With right sides together, layer the 5-1/4-inch **LIGHT GOLD** and **MEDIUM BROWN FLORAL** squares in pairs. Press together, but do not sew. Cut layered squares diagonally into quarters to make 8 sets of layered triangles (you will have 2 extra sets).

Step 4 Stitch along **bias** edge of each triangle set being careful not to stretch triangles; press. Be sure to sew along the same **bias** edge of each triangle set. Sew triangle units together in pairs; press. <u>At this point each hourglass block should measure 4-1/2-inches square.</u> Make 3 hourglass blocks. Sew blocks together; press.

<u>At this point the hourglass unit should measure 4-1/2 x 12-1/2-inches.</u>

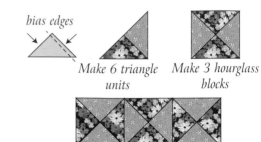

bias edges

Make 6 triangle units   *Make 3 hourglass blocks*

Make 1

Step 5 Sew 1-1/2 x 7-1/2-inch **ROSE/GOLD FLORAL** rectangle to left edge of 7-1/2-inch **LARGE BROWN FLORAL** square; press. Sew 1-1/2 x 8-1/2-inch **ROSE/GOLD FLORAL** rectangle to bottom edge of unit; press. <u>At this point the unit should measure 8-1/2-inches square.</u>

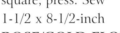

Make 1

Step 6 Sew Step 5 unit to right edge of Step 2 unit; press. <u>At this point the unit should measure 8-1/2 x 12-1/2-inches.</u>

Step 2   *Step 5*

Make 1

Step 7 Sew Step 4 unit to bottom edge of Step 6 unit; press. <u>At this point the block should measure 12-1/2-inches square.</u>

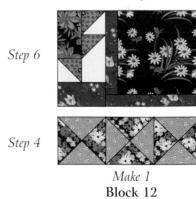

Step 6

Step 4

Make 1
Block 12

Quilt Center

Step 1 Referring to quilt center assembly diagram for block placement, lay out blocks in 4 horizontal rows with 3 blocks in each row. Sew blocks together in each row. Press seam allowances in alternating directions by rows so seams will fit snugly together with less bulk.

Step 2 Pin block rows together and sew. Press seam allowances in one direction. At this point quilt center should measure 36-1/2 x 48-1/2-inches.

Quilt Center Assembly Diagram

Borders

Note: *Yardage given allows for* **TONAL ROSE FLORAL,** **LIGHT GOLD PRINT,** *and* **GOLD FLORAL** *narrow border strips to be cut on crosswise grain. Diagonally piece the strips as needed, referring to* **Diagonal Piecing** *instructions on page 154. Yardage given allows for* **ROSE/GOLD FLORAL** *wide border strips to be cut on lengthwise grain (a couple extra inches are allowed for trimming). Read through* **Border** *instructions on page 153 for general instructions on adding borders.*

Cutting

From **TONAL ROSE FLORAL**:
- Cut 5, 2-1/2 x 44-inch inner border strips

From **LIGHT GOLD PRINT**:
- Cut 5, 1-1/2 x 44-inch first middle border strips

From **GOLD FLORAL**:
- Cut 6, 2-1/2 x 44-inch second middle border strips

From **ROSE/GOLD FLORAL:**—cut on lengthwise grain:
- Cut 2, 8-1/2 x 81-inch side outer border strips
- Cut 2, 8-1/2 x 50-inch top/bottom outer border strips

Attaching Borders

Step 1 Attach 2-1/2-inch wide **TONAL ROSE FLORAL** inner border strips.

Step 2 Attach 1-1/2-inch wide **LIGHT GOLD PRINT** first middle border strips.

Step 3 Attach 2-1/2-inch wide **GOLD FLORAL** second middle border strips.

Step 4 Attach 8-1/2-inch wide **ROSE/GOLD FLORAL** outer border strips.

Putting It All Together

Cut 3-3/4 yard length of backing fabric in half crosswise to make 2, 1-7/8 yard lengths. Refer to **Finishing the Quilt** on page 154 for complete instructions. Our quilt was quilted with an allover design.

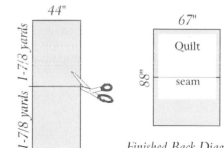

Finished Back Diagram

Binding

Cutting

From **MEDIUM GREEN PRINT**:
- Cut 7, 2-3/4 x 44-inch strips

Sew binding to quilt using a 3/8-inch seam allowance. This measurement will produce a 1/2-inch wide finished double binding. Refer to **Binding** and **Diagonal Piecing** on page 154 for complete instructions.

Crazy Quilt Puzzle Quilt

62 x 74-inches

Color Option—Autumn

Color Option—Winter

Crazy Quilt Puzzle Quilt Half-size Option

Thimbleberries® Basic Half-sizing

Half-sizing squares

Example One:

If your cut size is 4-1/2",
subtract the (2) seam allowances (1/4" each side). 4-1/2" minus 1/2" equals 4"... divide that in half which equals 2", then add the (2) seam allowances back on...2" plus 1/2" equals 2-1/2" <u>which is your new cut size.</u>

Example Two:

If your cut size is 1-1/2",
subtract the (2) seam allowances (1/4" each side). 1-1/2" minus 1/2" equals 1"... divide that in half which equals 1/2", then add the (2) seam allowances back on...1/2" plus 1/2" equals 1" <u>which is your new cut size.</u>

Half-sizing triangle-pieced squares

Example One:

If your cut size is 6-7/8",
subtract 7/8". 6-7/8" minus 7/8" equals 6"... divide that in half which equals 3",then add the 7/8" back on...3" plus 7/8" equals <u>3-7/8" which is your new cut size.</u>

Example Two:

If your cut size is 7-7/8",
subtract 7/8". 7-7/8" minus 7/8" equals 7"... divide that in half which equals 3-1/2",then add the 7/8" back on...3-1/2" plus 7/8" equals 4-3/8" <u>which is your new cut size.</u>

Hometown Christmas

*B*e inspired by heartwarming symbols expressing
the holiday spirit of home and family in the classic
Hometown Christmas Quilt Collection. Block-by-block,
messages of comfort, welcome, gift-giving, and sharing are
added until your special holiday quilt is completed.

Choose to quilt the heirloom bed quilt with its
companion pillows and shams or add a small
touch of Christmas spirit to a festive holiday table
with the December Dusk Runner. Hometown
Christmas is an enduring holiday collection you'll be
delighted to display.

HOMETOWN CHRISTMAS QUILT

100 x 112-inches

Fabrics & Supplies

1-3/8 yards **MEDIUM GOLD PRINT**

2 yards **BEIGE PRINT**

3/4 yard **DARK BLUE PRINT**

2-1/8 yards **BEIGE FLORAL**

1/2 yard **LIGHT GREEN PRINT**

2/3 yard **MEDIUM GREEN PRINT**

3/4 yard **DARK GREEN PRINT**

5/8 yard **BROWN PRINT #1**

5/8 yard **RED PRINT #1**

5/8 yard **MEDIUM BLUE PRINT**

1 yard **DARK GOLD PRINT**

1-1/4 yards **BLACK PRINT**
for inner border, corner squares

4-1/4 yards **RED PRINT #2**
for lattice strips, outer border

1/2 yard **BROWN PRINT #2** for quilt center

1 yard **BROWN PRINT #2** for binding

9 yards of 44-inch wide backing

OR

3-1/3 yards of 108-inch wide backing

quilt batting, at least 106 x 118-inches

*Before beginning this project,
read through* **Getting Started** *on page 145.*

Hometown Christmas
Hourglass Blocks

Make 15 hourglass blocks

Cutting

From **MEDIUM GOLD PRINT** and **BEIGE PRINT**:
• Cut 2, 7-1/4 x 44-inch strips from each fabric

Piecing

Step 1   With right sides together, layer 7-1/4-inch **MEDIUM GOLD** and **BEIGE PRINT** strips together in pairs. Press together, but do not sew. Cut layered strips into squares. Cut layered squares diagonally into quarters to make 32 sets of triangles. (There will be 2 extra sets of triangles.)

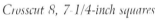

Crosscut 8, 7-1/4-inch squares

Step 2   Stitch 1/4-inch along the same **bias** edge of each pair of triangles being careful not to stretch triangles; press. Sew triangle sets together in pairs to make hourglass blocks; press. <u>At this point each hourglass block should measure 6-1/2-inches square.</u>

Bias edges

*Make 30
triangle sets*

*Make 15
hourglass blocks*

Step 3   Sew hourglass blocks together in pairs to make 3 hourglass block units; press and set aside. Set remaining hourglass blocks aside.

*Make 3 hourglass block
units (set aside)*

*Set 9 hourglass
blocks aside*

Hometown Christmas

Pinwheel Blocks
8-Pointed Star Block

Make 11 pinwheel blocks
Make 1, 8-pointed star block

Cutting

From **DARK BLUE PRINT**:
- Cut 1 to 2, 4-1/2 x 44-inch strips. From strips cut:
  1, 4-1/2-inch square
  8, 2-1/2 x 4-1/2-inch rectangles
  8, 2-1/2-inch squares
- Cut 2 to 3, 3-7/8 x 44-inch strips

From **BEIGE FLORAL**:
- Cut 2 to 3, 3-7/8 x 44-inch strips
- Cut 2, 2-1/2 x 44-inch strips. From strips cut:
  4, 2-1/2 x 4-1/2-inch rectangles
  16, 2-1/2-inch squares

Piecing Pinwheel Blocks

Step 1 With right sides together, layer 3-7/8 x 44-inch **DARK BLUE** and **BEIGE FLORAL** strips in pairs. Press together, but do not sew. Cut layered strips into squares. Cut layered squares diagonally in half to make 44 sets of triangles. Stitch 1/4-inch from diagonal edge of each set of triangles; press.

Crosscut 22, 3-7/8-inch squares   *Make 44, 3-1/2-inch triangle-pieced squares*

Step 2 Sew triangle-pieced squares together in pairs; press. Sew pairs together to make pinwheel blocks. <u>At this point each pinwheel block should measure 6-1/2-inches square.</u>

Make 22

Make 11 pinwheel blocks

Step 3 Sew together 9 pinwheel blocks and 9 hourglass blocks in pairs; press. Set units aside. Sew together 2 pinwheel blocks; press. Set units aside.

Make 9 (set aside)   *Make 1 (set aside)*

Piecing 8-Pointed Star Block

Step 1 Position a 2-1/2-inch **DARK BLUE** square on the corner of a 2-1/2 x 4-1/2-inch **BEIGE FLORAL** rectangle. Draw diagonal line on square; stitch, trim, and press. Repeat this process at opposite corner of rectangle to make star point units; press.

Make 4 star point units

Step 2 Sew star point units to top/bottom edges of 4-1/2-inch **DARK BLUE** square; press. Sew 2-1/2-inch **BEIGE FLORAL** squares to both edges of star point units; press. Sew the units to side edges of square; press. <u>At this point star unit should measure 8-1/2-inches square.</u>

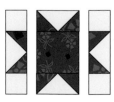

Make 1 star unit

Step 3 Position a 2-1/2-inch **BEIGE FLORAL** square on right corner of a 2-1/2 x 4-1/2-inch **DARK BLUE** rectangle. Draw diagonal line on square; stitch, trim, and press. Make 4 units. Position a 2-1/2-inch **BEIGE FLORAL** square on left corner of a 2-1/2 x 4-1/2-inch **DARK BLUE** rectangle. Note direction of stitching line. Draw diagonal line on square; stitch, trim, and press. Make 4 units.

Make 4   *Make 4*

Step 4 Sew Step 3 units together in pairs; press. <u>At this point each unit should measure 2-1/2 x 8-1/2-inches.</u>

Make 4

Step 5 Sew Step 4 units to top/bottom edges of star unit; press. Sew 2-1/2-inch **BEIGE FLORAL** squares to both edges of remaining Step 4 units; press. Sew the units to side edges of star unit; press. <u>At this point the 8-pointed star block should measure 12-1/2 inches square.</u> Referring to diagram, sew hourglass blocks to both side edges of star block; press. <u>At this point the star/hourglass section should measure 12-1/2 x 24-1/2-inches.</u>

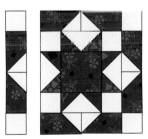
Make 1 8-pointed star block

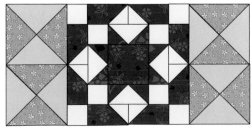
Make 1 star/hourglass section

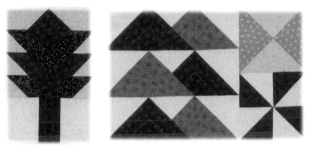

Hometown Christmas

Wreath Block
Tree Blocks (#1, #2, #3)
Holly Block

Cutting

Make 1 wreath block
Make 1 each of tree block #1, #2, & #3
Make 1 holly block

From **LIGHT GREEN PRINT**:
- Cut 1, 4-7/8 x 44-inch strip. From strip cut:
  2, 4-7/8-inch squares
  1, 4-1/2 x 8-1/2-inch rectangle
  4, 2-7/8-inch squares
- Cut 2, 2-1/2 x 44-inch strips. From strips cut:
  20, 2-1/2-inch squares

From **BEIGE FLORAL**:
- Cut 1, 4-7/8 x 44-inch strip. From strip cut:
  3, 4-7/8-inch squares

Hometown Christmas Quilt

3, 4-1/2-inch squares
4, 3-1/2 x 4-1/2-inch rectangles
• Cut 2, 2-1/2 x 44-inch strips. From strips cut:
8, 2-1/2 x 4-1/2-inch rectangles
4, 2-1/2-inch squares

From MEDIUM GREEN PRINT:
• Cut 1, 4-7/8 x 44-inch strip. From strip cut:
1, 4-7/8-inch square
2, 4-1/2 x 8-1/2-inch rectangles
• Cut 3, 2-1/2 x 44-inch strips. From strips cut:
11, 2-1/2 x 4-1/2-inch rectangles
16, 2-1/2-inch squares

From DARK GREEN PRINT:
• Cut 1, 4-7/8 x 44-inch strip. From strip cut:
1, 4-7/8-inch square
4, 2-7/8-inch squares
• Cut 2, 2-1/2 x 44-inch strips. From strips cut:
7, 2-1/2 x 4-1/2-inch rectangles
18, 2-1/2-inch squares

From BEIGE PRINT:
• Cut 1, 4-7/8 x 44-inch strip. From strip cut:
1, 4-7/8-inch square
8, 2-7/8-inch squares
• Cut 4, 2-1/2 x 44-inch strips. From strips cut:
18, 2-1/2 x 4-1/2-inch rectangles
26, 2-1/2-inch squares

From BROWN PRINT #1:
• Cut 1, 2-1/2 x 44-inch strip. From strip cut:
2, 2-1/2 x 4-1/2-inch rectangles

From RED PRINT #1:
• Cut 1, 2-1/2 x 44-inch strip. From strip cut:
2-1/2-inch squares

Piecing Wreath Block

Step 1 With right sides together, position 2-1/2-inch **LIGHT GREEN** squares on 2 opposite corners of the 4-1/2-inch **BEIGE FLORAL** square. Draw diagonal line on 2-1/2-inch squares; stitch on line. Trim seam allowance to 1/4-inch; press. Repeat this process at the 2 opposite corners of **BEIGE FLORAL** square; press.

Make 1

Step 2 Position a 2-1/2-inch **LIGHT GREEN** square on the corner of a 2-1/2 x 4-1/2-inch **MEDIUM GREEN** rectangle. Draw diagonal line on square; stitch, trim, and press. Repeat this process at opposite corner of rectangle.

Make 4

Step 3 Position a 2-1/2-inch **MEDIUM GREEN** square on the corner of a 2-1/2 x 4-1/2-inch **BEIGE FLORAL** rectangle. Draw diagonal line on square; stitch, trim, and press. Repeat this process at opposite corner of rectangle. Sew Step 2 units to bottom edge of the units; press.

Make 4   *Step 2*

Make 4

Step 4 Sew Step 3 units to top/bottom edges of Step 1 unit; press.

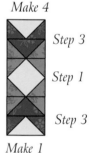

Step 3

Step 1

Step 3

Make 1

Step 5 Sew together 4, 2-1/2-inch **BEIGE FLORAL** and **MEDIUM GREEN** squares in pairs; press. Sew a 2-1/2 x 4-1/2-inch **BEIGE FLORAL** rectangle to right edge of unit; press. Make 4 units.

Make 4

Step 6 Sew Step 5 units to edges of remaining Step 3 units; press. Sew these units to side edges of Step 4 unit; press. <u>At this point wreath block should measure 12-1/2-inches square</u>.

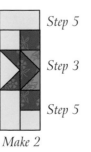

Step 5

Step 3

Step 5

Make 2

Make 1 wreath block

Piecing Tree Block #1

Step 1 With right sides together, layer 4-7/8-inch **DARK GREEN** and **BEIGE PRINT** squares. Press together, but do not sew. Cut layered square diagonally in half to make 2 sets of triangles. Stitch 1/4-inch from diagonal edge of each set of triangles; press.

Make 2, 4-1/2-inch triangle-pieced squares

Step 2 Position 2-1/2-inch **MEDIUM GREEN** squares on **DARK GREEN** corner of each triangle-pieced square. Draw diagonal line on **MEDIUM GREEN** square; stitch, trim, and press. Make 2 units. Sew units together; press.

Make 2   *Make 1*

Step 3 Position a 2-1/2-inch **BEIGE PRINT** square on left corner of a 2-1/2 x 4-1/2-inch **MEDIUM GREEN** rectangle. Draw diagonal line on square; stitch, trim, and press. Repeat this process at the opposite corner of the rectangle using a 2-1/2-inch **DARK GREEN** square; press.

Make 1

Step 4 Position a 2-1/2-inch **DARK GREEN** square on left corner of a 2-1/2 x 4-1/2-inch **MEDIUM GREEN** rectangle. Draw diagonal line on square; stitch, trim, and press. Repeat this process at the opposite corner of the rectangle using a 2-1/2-inch **BEIGE PRINT** square; press.

Make 1

Step 5 Sew together Step 3 and Step 4 units; press.

Step 3   *Step 4*

 *Make 1*

Step 6 Position a 2-1/2-inch **BEIGE PRINT** square on left corner of a 2-1/2 x 4-1/2-inch **DARK GREEN** rectangle. Draw diagonal line on square; stitch, trim, and press. Repeat this process at opposite corner of rectangle using a 2-1/2-inch **MEDIUM GREEN** square; press.

Make 1

Step 7 Position a 2-1/2-inch **MEDIUM GREEN** square on left corner of a 2-1/2 x 4-1/2-inch **DARK GREEN** rectangle. Draw diagonal line on square; stitch, trim, and press. Repeat this process at opposite corner of rectangle using a 2-1/2-inch **BEIGE PRINT** square; press.

Make 1

Step 8 Sew together Step 6 and Step 7 units; press.

Step 6   *Step 7*

 *Make 1*

Step 9 To make trunk unit, sew 3-1/2 x 4-1/2-inch **BEIGE FLORAL** rectangles to both side edges of 2-1/2 x 4-1/2-inch **BROWN #1** rectangle; press.

Make 1

Step 10 Sew together the Step 2, 5, 8, and 9 units; press. <u>At this point tree block #1 should measure 8-1/2 x 12-1/2-inches.</u>

Step 2

Step 5

Step 8

Step 9

Make 1 tree block #1

Step 11 Referring to diagram, sew together wreath block, tree block #1, and a pinwheel/hourglass unit; press. At this point wreath/tree #1/pinwheel/hourglass section should measure 12-1/2 x 26-1/2-inches.

Make 1 wreath/tree #1/pinwheel/hourglass section

Piecing Tree Block #2

Step 1 With right sides together, position a 2-1/2 x 4-1/2-inch **BEIGE PRINT** rectangle on the corner of a 2-1/2 x 4-1/2-inch **MEDIUM GREEN** rectangle; press. Draw diagonal line on **BEIGE** rectangle; stitch, trim, and press. Repeat this process at opposite corner of **MEDIUM GREEN** rectangle. At this point the unit should measure 2-1/2 x 8-1/2-inches.

Make 1

Step 2 Position a 2-1/2 x 4-1/2-inch **DARK GREEN** rectangle on the corner of a 2-1/2 x 4-1/2-inch **MEDIUM GREEN** rectangle; press. Draw a diagonal line on **DARK GREEN** rectangle; stitch, trim, and press. Repeat this process at opposite corner of **MEDIUM GREEN** rectangle. Position 2-1/2-inch **BEIGE PRINT** squares on the corners of the unit. Draw diagonal lines on squares; stitch, trim, and press. At this point each unit should measure 2-1/2 x 8-1/2-inches.

Make 2

Step 3 Position a 2-1/2 x 4-1/2-inch **MEDIUM GREEN** rectangle on the corner of a 2-1/2 x 4-1/2-inch **DARK GREEN** rectangle, press. Draw diagonal line on **MEDIUM GREEN** rectangle; stitch, trim, and press. Repeat this process at opposite corner of **DARK GREEN** rectangle. Position 2-1/2-inch **BEIGE PRINT** squares on the corners of the unit. Draw diagonal lines on squares; stitch, trim, and press. At this point the unit should measure 2-1/2 x 8-1/2-inches.

Make 1

Step 4 To make trunk unit, sew 3-1/2 x 4-1/2-inch **BEIGE FLORAL** rectangles to both side edges of a 2-1/2 x 4-1/2-inch **BROWN #1** rectangle; press.

Make 1

Step 5 Sew together Step 1, Step 2, Step 3, and Step 4 units; press. At this point tree block #2 should measure 8-1/2 x 12-1/2-inches. Set tree block aside.

Step 1
Step 2
Step 3
Step 2
Step 4

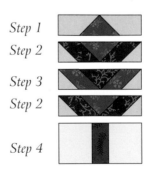

Make 1 tree block #2

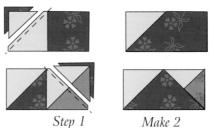

Piecing Tree Block #3

Step 1 With right sides together, layer 2, 4-7/8-inch **LIGHT GREEN** and **BEIGE FLORAL** squares together in pairs. Press together, but do not sew. Cut layered squares diagonally in half to make 4 sets of triangles. Stitch 1/4-inch from diagonal edge of each set of triangles; press.

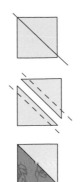

Make 4, 4-1/2-inch triangle-pieced squares

Step 2 With right sides together, layer 1, 4-7/8-inch **MEDIUM GREEN** and **BEIGE FLORAL** square together. Press together, but do not sew. Cut layered square diagonally in half to make 2 sets of triangles. Stitch 1/4-inch from diagonal edge of each set of triangles; press.

Make 2, 4-1/2 inch triangle-pieced squares

Step 3 Sew Step 1 triangle-pieced squares to top/bottom edges of 1 of the Step 2 triangle-pieced squares; press. <u>At this point unit should measure 4-1/2 x 12-1/2-inches.</u>

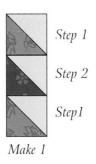

Step 1

Step 2

Step 1

Make 1

Step 4 Position a 4-1/2-inch **BEIGE FLORAL** square on left corner of 4-1/2 x 8-1/2-inch **MEDIUM GREEN** rectangle. Draw diagonal line on square; stitch on line. Trim seam allowance to 1/4-inch; press. Position a Step 1 triangle-pieced square on right corner of rectangle.

Draw diagonal line on pieced square; stitch, trim, and press.

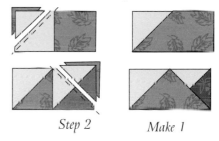

Step 1   *Make 2*

Step 5 Position a 4-1/2-inch **BEIGE FLORAL** square on left corner of 4-1/2 x 8-1/2-inch **LIGHT GREEN** rectangle. Draw diagonal line on square; stitch, trim, and press. Position a Step 2 triangle-pieced square on right corner of rectangle. Draw diagonal line on pieced square; stitch, trim, and press.

Step 2   *Make 1*

Step 6 Sew together Step 4 and Step 5 units; press. Sew Step 3 unit to right edge of unit; press. <u>At this point tree block #3 should measure 12-1/2 inches square.</u>

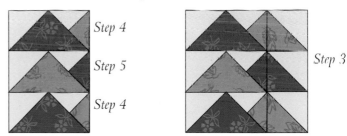

Step 4

Step 5

Step 4

Step 3

Make 1 tree block #3

Step 7 Referring to diagram, sew pinwheel/hourglass unit to tree block #3; press. <u>At this point tree #3/pinwheel/hourglass section should measure 12-1/2 x 18-1/2-inches.</u>

Make 1, tree #3/pinwheel/hourglass section

Piecing Holly Block

Step 1 With right sides together, layer 4 of the 2-7/8-inch **LIGHT GREEN** and **BEIGE PRINT** squares together in pairs. Press together, but do not sew. Cut layered squares diagonally in half to make 8 sets of triangles. Stitch 1/4-inch from diagonal edge of each set of triangles; press.

 *Make 8, 2-1/2-inch triangle-pieced squares*

Step 2 Repeat Step 1 using 4 of the 2-7/8-inch **DARK GREEN** and **BEIGE PRINT** squares to make 8 triangle-pieced squares.

 *Make 8, 2-1/2-inch triangle-pieced squares*

Step 3 With right sides together, position a 2-1/2-inch **DARK GREEN** square on right corner of a 2-1/2 x 4-1/2-inch **BEIGE PRINT** rectangle. Draw diagonal line on square; stitch, trim, and press. Make 8 units. Sew a Step 1 triangle-pieced square to left edge of each unit; press. <u>At this point each unit should measure 2-1/2 x 6-1/2-inches</u>.

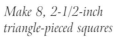

Make 8   *Make 8*

Step 4 Position a 2-1/2-inch **DARK GREEN** square on left corner of a 2-1/2 x 4-1/2-inch **BEIGE PRINT** rectangle. Draw diagonal line on square; stitch, trim, and press. Repeat this process at opposite corner of rectangle using 2-1/2-inch **LIGHT GREEN** squares. Make 8 units. Sew 2-1/2-inch **BEIGE PRINT** squares to right edge of each unit; press. <u>At this point each unit should measure 2-1/2 x 6-1/2-inches</u>.

Make 8   *Make 8*

Step 5 Sew together a 2-1/2-inch **BEIGE PRINT** square, a Step 2 triangle-pieced square, and a 2-1/2-inch **RED #1** square; press. <u>At this point each unit should measure 2-1/2 x 6-1/2-inches</u>.

Make 8

Step 6 Referring to diagram for placement, sew together Step 3, Step 4, and Step 5 units; press. <u>At this point each holly unit should measure 6-1/2 x 24-1/2-inches</u>.

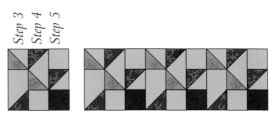

Make 2 holly units

Step 7 Referring to diagram for placement, sew Step 6 holly units together; press. <u>At this point holly block should measure 12-1/2 x 24-1/2-inches</u>. Set holly block aside.

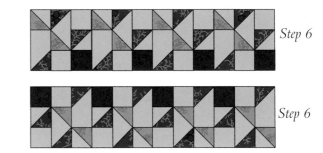

Make 1 holly block

Hometown Christmas

Fence Block
Blue Roof House Block

Cutting

Make 1 fence block
Make 1 blue roof house block

From **MEDIUM BLUE PRINT**:
- Cut 1, 4-1/2 x 44-inch strip. From strip cut:
  3, 4-1/2 x 6-1/2-inch rectangles
  3, 4-1/2-inch squares
- Cut 3, 2-1/2 x 44-inch strips. From strips cut:
  1, 2-1/2 x 6-1/2-inch rectangle
  6, 2-1/2 x 4-1/2-inch rectangles
  26, 2-1/2 inch squares

From **BEIGE PRINT**:
- Cut 1, 2-1/2 x 44-inch strip. From strip cut:
  6, 2-1/2 x 6-1/2-inch rectangles

From **DARK GOLD PRINT**:
- Cut 2, 2-1/2 x 44-inch strips. From strips cut:
  5, 2-1/2 x 6-1/2-inch rectangles
  8, 2-1/2-inch squares

From **BEIGE FLORAL**:
- Cut 1, 4-1/2 x 44-inch strip. From strip cut:
  2, 4-1/2-inch squares
  1, 2-1/2 x 8-1/2-inch rectangle
  2, 2-1/2 x 4-1/2-inch rectangles
- Cut 1, 2-1/2 x 44-inch strip. From strip cut:
  6, 2-1/2 x 6-1/2-inch rectangles

From **BROWN PRINT #1**:
- Cut 1, 4-1/2 x 44-inch strip. From strip cut:
  1, 4-1/2 x 8-1/2-inch rectangle

From **LIGHT GREEN PRINT**:
- Cut 1, 2-1/2 x 44-inch strip. From strip cut:
  4, 2-1/2 x 6-1/2-inch rectangles
  4, 2-1/2-inch squares

From **BLACK PRINT**:
- Cut 1, 2-1/2 x 44-inch strip. From strip cut:
  1, 2-1/2 x 4-1/2-inch rectangle
  2, 2-1/2-inch squares

Piecing Fence Block

Step 1   Position a 2-1/2-inch **DARK GOLD** square on left corner of a 2-1/2 x 4-1/2-inch **MEDIUM BLUE** rectangle. Draw diagonal line on square; stitch on line. Trim seam allowance to 1/4-inch; press. Sew a 2-1/2-inch **MEDIUM BLUE** square to left edge of unit; press. <u>At this point each unit should measure 2-1/2 x 6-1/2-inches.</u>

Make 6

Step 2   Position 2-1/2-inch **MEDIUM BLUE** squares on both corners of a 2-1/2 x 6-1/2-inch **DARK GOLD** rectangle. Draw diagonal line on squares; stitch, trim, and press.

Make 3

Step 3   Sew Step 1 units to top/bottom edges of Step 2 units; press. <u>At this point each star unit should measure 6-1/2-inches square.</u>

Step 1
Step 2
Step 1

Make 3 star units

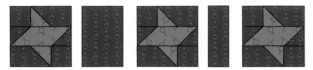

Step 4 Sew together Step 3 star units, 4-1/2 x 6-1/2-inch **MEDIUM BLUE** rectangle, and 2-1/2 x 6-1/2-inch **MEDIUM BLUE** rectangle; press. <u>At this point star unit should measure 6-1/2 x 24-1/2-inches</u>.

Make 1 star unit

Step 5 Position a 2-1/2-inch **MEDIUM BLUE** square on top corner of a 2-1/2 x 6-1/2-inch **BEIGE PRINT** rectangle. Draw diagonal line on square; stitch, trim, and press.

Make 6

Step 6 Position a 2-1/2-inch **MEDIUM BLUE** square on top corner of a 2-1/2 x 6-1/2-inch **BEIGE FLORAL** rectangle. Notice direction of sewing line. Draw diagonal line on square; stitch, trim, and press.

Make 6

Step 7 Sew together Step 5 and Step 6 units in pairs; press. Sew pairs together to make fence unit; press. <u>At this point fence unit should measure 6-1/2 x 24-1/2-inches</u>.

Step 5
Step 6

Make 6

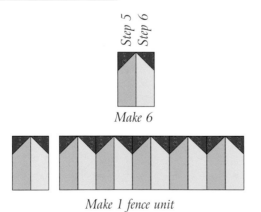

Make 1 fence unit

Step 8 Sew star unit to top edge of fence unit; press. Sew pinwheel/hourglass unit to left edge and hourglass unit to right edge; press. <u>At this point fence/pinwheel/hourglass section should measure 12-1/2 x 36-1/2-inches</u>.

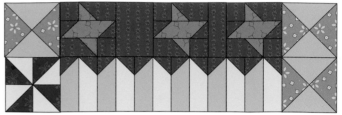

Make 1 fence/pinwheel/hourglass section

Piecing Blue Roof House Block

Step 1 Sew 2-1/2-inch **MEDIUM BLUE** squares to both ends of the 2-1/2 x 8-1/2-inch **BEIGE FLORAL** rectangle. Sew 2 of the 2-1/2 x 4-1/2-inch **BEIGE FLORAL** rectangles to both ends of unit; press. <u>At this point chimney unit should measure 2-1/2 x 20-1/2-inches</u>.

Make 1 chimney unit

Step 2 Position a 4-1/2-inch **BEIGE FLORAL** square on left edge of 4-1/2 x 6-1/2-inch **MEDIUM BLUE** rectangle. Draw diagonal line on square; stitch on the line. Trim seam allowance to 1/4-inch; press. Make 1 unit. Repeat this process to make another unit, positioning 4-1/2-inch **BEIGE FLORAL** square on right edge of 4-1/2 x 6-1/2-inch **MEDIUM BLUE** rectangle. Make 1 unit.

Make 1 for left side   *Make 1 for right side*

Step 3   Position a 4-1/2-inch **MEDIUM BLUE** square on the corner of 4-1/2 x 8-1/2-inch **BROWN #1** rectangle. Draw diagonal line on square; stitch, trim, and press. Repeat this process at opposite corner of rectangle; press.

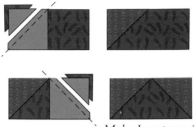

Make 1 center unit

Step 4   Sew Step 2 units to both side edges of Step 3 center unit; press. Sew Step 1 chimney unit to top edge; press. At this point roof unit should measure 6-1/2 x 20-1/2-inches.

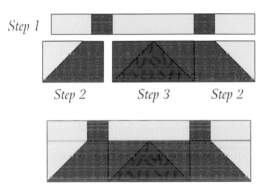

Make 1 roof unit

Step 5   Sew 2-1/2-inch **LIGHT GREEN** squares to top/bottom edges of 2-1/2-inch **BLACK** squares; press. Make 2 units. Sew 2-1/2 x 6-1/2-inch **LIGHT GREEN** rectangles to both side edges of units; press. At this point each window unit should measure 6-1/2-inches square.

Make 2 window units

Step 6   Position a 2-1/2-inch **DARK GOLD** square on the corner of 2-1/2 x 4-1/2-inch **BLACK** rectangle. Draw diagonal line on square; stitch, trim, and press. Repeat this process at opposite corner of rectangle; press. Sew unit to top edge of 4-1/2-inch **MEDIUM BLUE** square; press. Sew 2-1/2 x 6-1/2-inch **DARK GOLD** rectangles to both side edges of door unit; press. At this point door unit should measure 6-1/2 x 8-1/2-inches.

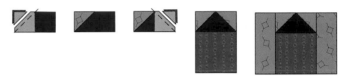

Make 1   Make 1 door unit

Step 7   Sew Step 5 window units to both side edges of Step 6 door unit; press. Sew Step 4 roof unit to top edge of house unit; press. At this point blue roof house block should measure 12-1/2 x 20-1/2-inches.

Make 1 blue roof house

Step 6

Hometown Christmas
Red Roof House Block
Gift Package Block
Cardinal Block

Cutting

Make 1 red roof house block
Make 1 gift package block
Make 1 cardinal block

From **RED PRINT #1**:
- Cut 1, 8-1/2 x 44-inch strip. From strip cut:
  1, 8-1/2 x 12-1/2-inch rectangle
  2, 3-1/2 x 4-1/2-inch rectangles
  2, 2-7/8-inch squares
  2, 1-1/2 x 2-1/2-inch rectangles
  2, 1-1/2-inch squares
- Cut 1, 2-1/2 x 44-inch strip. From strip cut:
  4, 2-1/2 x 6-1/2-inch rectangles
  8, 2-1/2-inch squares

From **BROWN PRINT #1**:
- Cut 1, 3-1/2 x 44-inch strip. From strip cut:

2, 3-1/2 x 4-1/2-inch rectangles
1, 2-1/2 x 8-1/2-inch rectangle
2, 1-1/2 x 2-1/2-inch rectangles
2, 1-1/2-inch squares

From **BEIGE PRINT**:
- Cut 1, 4-1/2 x 44-inch strip. From strip cut:
  1, 4-1/2 x 8-1/2-inch rectangle
  1, 4-1/2-inch square
  1, 2-1/2 x 8-1/2-inch rectangle

From **MEDIUM GREEN PRINT**:
- Cut 1, 3-1/2 x 44-inch strip. From strip cut:
  2, 3-1/2 x 4-1/2-inch rectangles
  2, 2-1/2 x 4-1/2-inch rectangles
  2, 2-1/2-inch squares
  2, 1-1/2 x 2-1/2-inch rectangles
  2, 1-1/2-inch squares

From **BLACK PRINT**:
- Cut 1, 4-1/2-inch square

From **BEIGE FLORAL**:
- Cut 1, 2-7/8 x 44-inch strip. From strip cut:
  2, 2-7/8-inch squares
  1, 2-1/2 x 12-1/2-inch rectangle
  3, 2-1/2 x 6-1/2-inch rectangles
- Cut 3, 2-1/2 x 44-inch strips. From strips cut:
  6, 2-1/2 x 4-1/2-inch rectangles
  25, 2-1/2-inch squares
- Cut 3, 1-1/2 x 44-inch strips. From strips cut:
  8, 1-1/2 x 4-1/2-inch rectangles
  8, 1-1/2 x 3-1/2-inch rectangles
  8, 1-1/2 x 2-inch rectangles
  8, 1-1/2-inch squares

From **DARK GOLD PRINT**:
- Cut 1, 3-1/2 x 44-inch strip. From strip cut:
  16, 1-1/2 x 3-1/2-inch rectangles
  2, 2-1/2-inch squares
  8, 1-1/2-inch squares

From **MEDIUM GOLD PRINT**:
- Cut 2, 1-1/2 x 44-inch strips. From strips cut:
  8, 1-1/2 x 5-1/2-inch rectangles
  4, 1-1/2 x 4-1/2-inch rectangles

From **DARK GREEN PRINT**:
- Cut 1, 3-1/2 x 44-inch strip. From strip cut:
  2, 3-1/2 x 4-1/2-inch rectangles
  2, 1-1/2 x 2-1/2-inch rectangles
  2, 1-1/2-inch squares
- Cut 1 to 2, 2-1/2 x 44-inch strips. From strips cut:
  10, 2-1/2 x 4-1/2-inch rectangles

Piecing Red Roof House Block

Step 1 Sew together the 2-1/2 x 8-1/2-inch **BEIGE PRINT** and **BROWN #1** rectangles, and the 4-1/2 x 8-1/2-inch **BEIGE PRINT** rectangle; press. Referring to diagram for placement, position pieced square on left corner of 8-1/2 x 12-1/2-inch **RED #1** rectangle. Draw diagonal line on pieced square; stitch, trim, and press. Position 4-1/2-inch **BEIGE PRINT** square on upper right corner of unit. Draw diagonal line on square; stitch, trim, and press. At this point roof unit should measure 8-1/2 x 12-1/2-inches.

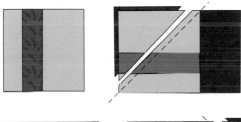

Make 1 roof unit

Step 2 Sew together a 2-1/2-inch **DARK GOLD** and **MEDIUM GREEN** square; press. Make 2 units. Referring to diagrams, sew a 2-1/2 x 4-1/2-inch **MEDIUM GREEN** rectangle to the side edge of each unit to make window units; press. Sew window units to both side edges of 4-1/2-inch **BLACK** square; press. At this point house unit should measure 4-1/2 x 12-1/2-inches.

Make 2   *Make 1 house unit*

Step 3 Sew Step 1 roof unit to Step 2 house unit; press. At this point red roof house block should measure 12-1/2-inches square.

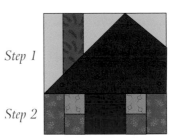

Step 1

Step 2

Make 1 red roof house block

Step 4 Sew pinwheel unit to left edge of house unit; press. At this point pinwheel/red roof house section should measure 12-1/2 x 18-1/2-inches.

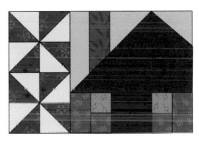

Make 1 pinwheel/red roof house section

Piecing Gift Package Block

Step 1 Position a 1-1/2 x 3-1/2-inch **BEIGE FLORAL** rectangle on left corner of 1-1/2 x 3-1/2-inch **DARK GOLD** rectangle. Draw diagonal line on **BEIGE FLORAL** rectangle; stitch, trim, and press. Position a 1-1/2 x 2-inch **BEIGE FLORAL** rectangle on right corner of **DARK GOLD** rectangle. Draw diagonal line on **BEIGE FLORAL** rectangle; stitch, trim, and press. At this point each unit should measure 1-1/2 x 6-inches.

Make 4

Step 2 Position a 1-1/2 x 2-inch **BEIGE FLORAL** rectangle on left corner of 1-1/2 x 3-1/2-inch **DARK GOLD** rectangle. Draw diagonal line on **BEIGE FLORAL** rectangle; stitch, trim, and press. Position a 1-1/2 x 3-1/2-inch **BEIGE FLORAL** rectangle on right corner of **DARK GOLD** rectangle. Draw diagonal line on **BEIGE FLORAL** rectangle; stitch, trim, and press. At this point each unit should measure 1-1/2 x 6-inches.

Make 4

Step 3 Sew together Step 1 and Step 2 units in pairs; press. At this point each unit should measure 1-1/2 x 11-1/2-inches.

Step 1   Step 2

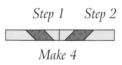

Make 4

Step 4 Position a 1-1/2-inch **BEIGE FLORAL** square on left corner of a 1-1/2 x 5-1/2-inch **MEDIUM GOLD** rectangle. Draw diagonal line on square; stitch, trim, and press. Make 8 units. Sew units to both side edges of a 1-1/2-inch **DARK GOLD** square; press. At this point each unit should measure 1-1/2 x 11-1/2-inches.

Make 8   Make 4

Step 5 Sew together Step 3 and Step 4 units in pairs; press. At this point each bow unit should measure 2-1/2 x 11-1/2-inches.

Step 3
Step 4

Make 4 bow units

Step 6 To make **DARK GREEN** package, position a 1-1/2 x 2-1/2-inch **DARK GREEN** rectangle on left corner of 1-1/2 x 3-1/2-inch **DARK GOLD** rectangle. Draw diagonal line on **DARK GREEN** rectangle; stitch, trim, and press. Repeat this process at right corner of **DARK GOLD** rectangle using a 1-1/2-inch **DARK GREEN** square. Sew a

3-1/2 x 4-1/2-inch **DARK GREEN** rectangle to bottom edge of unit; press. At this point unit should measure 4-1/2-inches square.

Make 1   *Make 1*

Step 7 Position a 1-1/2-inch **DARK GREEN** square on left corner of 1-1/2 x 3-1/2-inch **DARK GOLD** rectangle. Draw diagonal line on **DARK GREEN** square; stitch, trim, and press. Repeat this process at right corner of **DARK GOLD** rectangle using 1-1/2 x 2-1/2-inch **DARK GREEN** rectangle. Sew a 3-1/2 x 4-1/2-inch **DARK GREEN** rectangle to bottom edge of unit; press. At this point unit should measure 4-1/2-inches square.

Make 1   *Make 1*

Step 8 Sew together Step 6 unit, Step 7 unit, 1 of the 1-1/2 x 4-1/2-inch **MEDIUM GOLD** rectangles, and 2 of the 1-1/2 x 4-1/2-inch **BEIGE FLORAL** rectangles; press. Sew a Step 5 bow unit to top edge of package unit; press. At this point **DARK GREEN** package unit should measure 6-1/2 x 11-1/2-inches.

Step 6   Step 7   Step 5

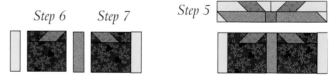

Make 1
dark green package

Step 9 To make **RED #1**, **BROWN #1**, and **MEDIUM GREEN** packages, repeat Step 6 through Step 8 using corresponding rectangles and squares.

Make 1   Make 1   Make 1 medium
red #1 package   brown #1 package   green package

Step 10 Sew together Step 8 and Step 9 packages; press. <u>At this point gift package block should measure 12-1/2 x 22-1/2-inches.</u>

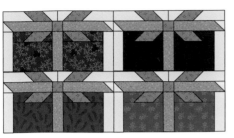

Make 1 gift package block

Piecing Cardinal Block

Step 1 Position a 2-1/2-inch **RED #1** square on the corner of a 2-1/2 x 4-1/2-inch **BEIGE FLORAL** rectangle. Draw diagonal line on square; stitch, trim, and press. Repeat this process at opposite corner of rectangle.

Make 4

Step 2 With right sides together, layer 2-7/8-inch **RED #1** and **BEIGE FLORAL** squares together in pairs. Press together, but do not sew. Cut layered squares diagonally in half to make 4 sets of triangles. Stitch 1/4-inch from diagonal edge of each set of triangles, press.

Make 4, 2-1/2-inch triangle-pieced squares

Step 3 Position a 1-1/2-inch **DARK GOLD** square on lower left corner of a 2-1/2-inch **BEIGE FLORAL** square. Draw diagonal line on **DARK GOLD** square; stitch, trim, and press.

 Make 1

Step 4 Position a 1-1/2-inch **DARK GOLD** square on lower left corner of a 2-1/2 x 6-1/2-inch **BEIGE FLORAL** rectangle. Draw diagonal line on square; stitch, trim, and press.

 *Make 1*

Step 5 Referring to diagram, sew together 2 of the Step 1 units, 2 of the Step 2 triangle-pieced squares, Step 3 unit, and Step 4 unit; press. <u>At this point unit should measure 2-1/2 x 20-1/2-inches.</u>

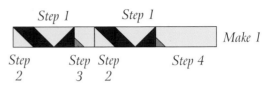

Step 6 Position 2-1/2-inch **BEIGE FLORAL** squares on both corners of a 2-1/2 x 6-1/2-inch **RED #1** rectangle. Draw diagonal line on squares; stitch, trim, and press.

Make 1

Step 7 Position a 2-1/2 x 4-1/2-inch **BEIGE FLORAL** rectangle on left corner of a 2-1/2 x 6-1/2-inch **RED #1** rectangle. Draw diagonal line on **BEIGE FLORAL** rectangle; stitch, trim, and press. Position a 2-1/2-inch **BEIGE FLORAL** square on right corner of unit. Draw diagonal line on square; stitch, trim, and press. Position a 1-1/2-inch **DARK GOLD** square on right corner of unit. Draw diagonal line on square; stitch, trim, and press. <u>At this point unit should measure 2-1/2 x 8-1/2-inches.</u>

Make 1

Step 8 Referring to diagram, sew together Step 6 unit, Step 7 unit, 1 of the Step 1 units, and 1 of the Step 2 triangle-pieced squares; press. <u>At this point unit should measure 2-1/2 x 20-1/2-inches.</u>

From **RED PRINT #1**:
- Cut 1, 2-1/2 x 44-inch strip. From strip cut: 2, 2-1/2 x 7-1/2-inch rectangles
- Cut 1, 1-1/2 x 44-inch strip. From strip cut: 7, 1-1/2 x 4-1/2-inch rectangles

From **DARK BLUE PRINT**:
- Cut 1, 2-1/2 x 44-inch strip. From strip cut: 2, 2-1/2 x 7-1/2-inch rectangles
  3, 1-1/2 x 4-1/2-inch rectangles

From **MEDIUM GREEN PRINT**:
- Cut 2, 2-1/2 x 44-inch strips.From strips cut: 4, 2-1/2 x 8-1/2-inch rectangles
  2, 2-1/2 x 7-1/2-inch rectangles
  2, 2-1/2 x 4-1/2-inch rectangles
  4, 2-1/2-inch squares
  3, 1-1/2 x 4-1/2-inch rectangles

Piecing Gold House Block #1

Step 1   Position a 6-1/2-inch **BROWN #1** square on bottom corner of a 6-1/2 x 8-1/2-inch **BEIGE PRINT** rectangle. Draw diagonal line on square; stitch on line. Trim seam allowance to 1/4-inch; press. Make 1 roof unit. Repeat this process to make another unit, reversing the direction of stitching line. Make 1 roof unit.

Make 1 roof unit for left side   *Make 1 roof unit for right side*

Step 2   Sew 1-1/2 x 2-1/2-inch **MEDIUM GOLD** rectangles to top/bottom edges of 2-1/2-inch **BLACK** square; press. Make 2 units. Referring to diagrams for placement, sew a 3-1/2 x 4-1/2-inch **MEDIUM GOLD** rectangle to the edge of each unit and sew a 1-1/2 x 4-1/2-inch **MEDIUM GOLD**

rectangle to the opposite edge of each unit, press. At this point each window unit should measure 4-1/2 x 6-1/2-inches.

Make 2   *Make 1 window unit for left side*   *Make 1 window unit for right side*

Step 3   Sew Step 1 roof units to top edge of Step 2 window units; press. At this point each side house unit should measure 6-1/2 x 12-1/2-inches.

left side Make 1   *right side Make 1*

Step 4   Position a 2-1/2-inch **MEDIUM GOLD** square on bottom corner of a 2-1/2 x 4-1/2-inch **BLACK** rectangle. Draw diagonal line on square; stitch, trim, and press. Make 1 unit. Repeat this process to make another unit, reversing the direction of stitching line. Make 1 unit. Sew the 2 units together; press. Sew unit to top edge of 4-1/2 x 8-1/2-inch **MEDIUM GOLD** rectangle; press. At this point center unit should measure 4-1/2 x 12-1/2-inches.

Make 1   *Make 1*

Make 1 center unit

Step 5 Sew Step 3 side house units to both side edges of Step 4 center unit; press. <u>At this point gold house block #1 should measure 12-1/2 x 16-1/2-inches.</u>

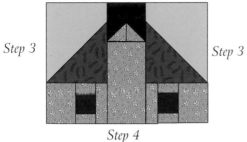

Step 3　　　　　　　　　　*Step 3*

Step 4

Make 1 gold house block #1

Piecing Gold House Block #2

Step 1 Position a 4-1/2-inch **BEIGE FLORAL** square on the corner of a 4-1/2 x 8-1/2-inch **DARK GOLD** rectangle. Draw a diagonal line on square; stitch on line. Trim seam allowance to 1/4-inch; press. Repeat this process at opposite corner of rectangle to make roof unit.

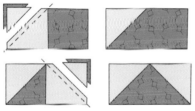

Make 1 roof unit

Step 2 Sew together 3 of the 1 x 2-1/2-inch **DARK GOLD** rectangles and 3 of the 2 x 2-1/2-inch **BLACK** rectangles; press. Make 2 window units. Sew together window units and 2-1/2 x 6-1/2-inch **DARK GOLD** rectangles; press. <u>At this point window unit should measure 6-1/2 x 8-1/2-inches.</u> Sew 2-1/2 x 8-1/2-inch **DARK GOLD** rectangle to left edge of window unit to make house unit;

press. Sew roof unit to top edge of house unit; press. <u>At this point house unit should measure 8-1/2 x 12-inches.</u>

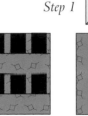

Step 1

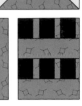

Make 2 window units

Make 1　　　*Make 1 house unit*

Step 3 Aligning long edges, sew together 2-1/2 x 8-1/2-inch **BEIGE FLORAL** and **BROWN #1** rectangles to make chimney unit; press. Position chimney unit on upper corner of 4-1/2 x 8-1/2-inch **DARK GOLD** rectangle. Draw a diagonal line on chimney unit; stitch, trim, and press. <u>At this point chimney unit should measure 4-1/2 x 12-1/2-inches.</u> Sew unit to right edge of house unit; press. <u>At this point gold house block #2 should measure 12-1/2-inches square.</u>

Make 1 chimney unit

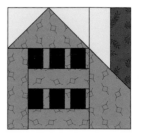

Make 1 gold house block #2

Piecing Row House Block

Step 1 With right sides together, position a 4-1/2-inch **BEIGE PRINT** square on the corner of a 4-1/2 x 8-1/2-inch **DARK GREEN** rectangle. Draw diagonal line on square; stitch, trim, and press. Repeat this process at opposite corner of rectangle; press. Make 1 **DARK GREEN** roof unit. Repeat this process with remaining **BEIGE PRINT** squares and 4-1/2 x 8-1/2-inch **MEDIUM BLUE** and **BROWN #1** rectangles. Make a total of 3 roof units.

Make 1 dark green, medium blue, and brown #1 roof unit

Step 2 Sew 1-1/2 x 2-1/2-inch **BLACK** rectangles to both side edges of 6 of the 2-1/2-inch **MEDIUM GOLD** squares to make window units; press.

 Make 6 window units

Step 3 To make **RED #1** house, sew the 3, 1-1/2 x 4-1/2-inch **RED #1** rectangles to 2 of the window units; press. Make 1 window unit. <u>At this point window unit should measure 4-1/2 x 7-1/2-inches.</u> Sew 2-1/2 x 7-1/2-inch **RED #1** rectangles to side edges of window unit; press. Sew 1-1/2 x 8-1/2-inch **DARK GREEN** rectangle to bottom edge of house unit; press. Sew **DARK GREEN** roof unit to top edge of house unit; press. <u>At this point **RED #1** house should measure 8-1/2 x 12-1/2-inches.</u>

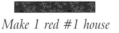

Make 1 window unit

Make 1 red #1 house

Step 4 To make **MEDIUM GREEN** house, sew the 3, 1-1/2 x 4-1/2-inch **MEDIUM GREEN** rectangles to 2 window units; press. Sew 2-1/2 x 7-1/2-inch **MEDIUM GREEN** rectangles to side edges of window unit; press. Sew 1-1/2 x 8-1/2-inch **MEDIUM BLUE** rectangle to bottom edge of house; press. Sew **MEDIUM BLUE** roof unit to top edge of house; press. <u>At this point **MEDIUM GREEN** house should measure 8-1/2 x 12-1/2-inches.</u>

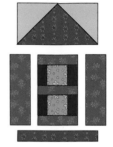

Make 1 window unit

Make 1 medium green house

Step 5 To make **DARK BLUE** house, sew the 3, 1-1/2 x 4-1/2-inch **DARK BLUE** rectangles to 2 window units; press. Sew 2-1/2 x 7-1/2-inch **DARK BLUE** rectangles to side edges of window unit; press. Sew 1-1/2 x 8-1/2-inch **BROWN #1** rectangle to bottom edge of house; press. Sew **BROWN #1** roof unit to top edge of house; press. <u>At this point **DARK BLUE** house should measure 8-1/2 x 12-1/2-inches.</u>

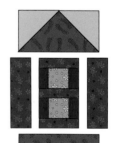

Make 1 window unit

Make 1 dark blue house

Step 6 Sew together an hourglass/pinwheel unit and the Step 3, Step 4, and Step 5 houses; press. At this point the pinwheel/hourglass/row house section should measure 12-1/2 x 30-1/2-inches.

Make 1 pinwheel/hourglass/row house section

Piecing Green House Block

Step 1 Position a 4-1/2-inch **DARK GOLD** square on the corner of a 4-1/2 x 8-1/2-inch **BROWN #1** rectangle. Draw diagonal line on square; stitch, trim, and press. Repeat this process at opposite corner of rectangle. Position 2-1/2-inch **BEIGE PRINT** squares on upper corners of the unit. Draw diagonal lines on squares; stitch, trim, and press. At this point each roof unit should measure 4-1/2 x 8-1/2-inches.

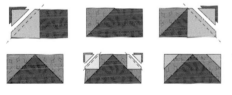

Make 2 roof units

Step 2 Position a 2-1/2-inch **MEDIUM GREEN** square on the corner of a 2-1/2 x 4-1/2-inch **BROWN #1** rectangle. Draw diagonal line on square; stitch, trim, and press. Repeat this process at opposite corner of rectangle.

Make 2

Step 3 Sew 1-1/2 x 4-1/2-inch **RED #1** rectangles to both side edges of a 2-1/2 x 4-1/2-inch **DARK GOLD** rectangle; press. Make 2 window units. Sew a Step 2 unit to each window unit and

sew a 2-1/2 x 4-1/2-inch **MEDIUM GREEN** rectangle to bottom edge; press. Sew 2-1/2 x 8-1/2-inch **MEDIUM GREEN** rectangles to both side edges of each window unit; press. At this point each window unit should measure 8-1/2-inches square.

Make 2   *Step 2*

Make 2   *Make 2 window units*

Step 4 Sew Step 1 roof units to top edge of each Step 3 window unit; press. At this point each side house unit should measure 8-1/2 x 12-1/2-inches.

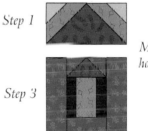

Step 1

Make 2 side house units

Step 3

Step 5 Position a 2-1/2-inch **BEIGE PRINT** square on the corner of a 2-1/2 x 4-1/2-inch **BLACK** rectangle. Draw diagonal line on square; stitch, trim, and press. Repeat this process at opposite corner of rectangle.

Make 1

Step 6 Position a 2-1/2-inch **BLACK** square on the corner of a 2-1/2 x 4-1/2-inch **DARK GOLD** rectangle. Draw diagonal line on square; stitch, trim, and press. Repeat this process at opposite corner of rectangle.

Make 1

Step 7 Position a 2-1/2-inch **DARK GOLD** square on the corner of a 2 1/2 x 4-1/2-inch **BLACK** rectangle. Draw diagonal line on square; stitch, trim, and press. Repeat this process at opposite corner of rectangle.

Make 1

Step 8 Sew together Step 5, Step 6, and Step 7 units; press. Sew a 4-1/2 x 6-1/2-inch **DARK GOLD** rectangle to bottom edge of roof unit; press. At this point center unit should measure 4-1/2 x 12-1/2-inches.

Step 5
Step 6
Step 7
Make 1 center unit

Step 9 Sew Step 4 side house units to both side edges of the Step 8 center unit; press. At this point green house block should measure 12-1/2 x 20-1/2-inches.

Step 4   Step 8   Step 4
Make 1 green house block

Borders and Lattice

Note: *Yardage given allows for lattice and border strips to be cut on crosswise grain. Diagonally piece strips as needed, referring to* **Diagonal Piecing** *instructions on page 154.*

Cutting

From **RED PRINT #2**:
• Cut 11, 8-1/2 x 44-inch outer border strips
• Cut 12, 4-1/2 x 44-inch lattice strips

From **BLACK PRINT**:
• Cut 1, 4-1/2 x 44-inch strip. From strip cut: 4, 4-1/2-inch corner squares
• Cut 9, 2-1/2 x 44-inch inner border strips

From **DARK GOLD PRINT, MEDIUM GOLD PRINT, BEIGE PRINT,** and **BEIGE FLORAL**:
• Cut 10, 1-1/2 x 44-inch strips from *each* fabric

From **BROWN PRINT #2**:
• Cut 6, 2-1/2 x 44-inch strips. From strips cut: 18, 2-1/2 x 12-1/2-inch rectangles

Quilt Center Assembly

Step 1 Referring to quilt assembly diagram for placement, sew together the prepared Sections, Units, and 2-1/2 x 12-1/2-inch **BROWN #2** rectangles to make 5 block rows; press. At this point each block row should measure 12-1/2 x 72-1/2-inches.

Step 2 Cut 6, 4-1/2-inch wide **RED #2** lattice strips to the block row length (72-1/2-inches long).

Step 3 Sew together the 5 block rows and the 6, 4-1/2 x 72-1/2-inch **RED #2** lattice strips. At this point quilt center should measure 72-1/2 x 84-1/2-inches.

Quilt Center Assembly Diagram

Assembling and Attaching Borders

Step 1   With pins, mark center points along all 4 sides of quilt. For top and bottom borders, measure quilt from left to right through the middle. This measurement will give you the most accurate measurement that will result in a "square" quilt.

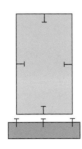

Step 2   Measure and mark border lengths and center points on the 2-1/2-inch wide **BLACK** strips cut for borders before sewing them on.

Step 3   Pin border strips to quilt matching pinned points on each of the borders and the quilt. Pin borders every 6 to 8-inches easing fabric to fit as necessary. This will prevent borders and quilt center from stretching while you are sewing them together. Stitch a 1/4-inch seam. Press seam allowances toward borders. Trim off excess border lengths.

Trim away excess fabric

Step 4   For side borders, measure quilt from top to bottom through the middle, including borders just added to determine length of side borders.

Step 5   Measure and mark the 2-1/2-inch wide **BLACK** side border lengths as you did for the top/bottom borders. Pin and stitch side border strips in place. Press and trim border strips even with borders just added.

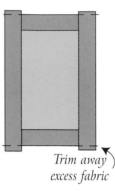

Trim away excess fabric

Step 6   Aligning long edges, sew together 1-1/2-inch wide **DARK GOLD**, **BEIGE PRINT**, **MEDIUM GOLD**, and **BEIGE FLORAL** strips. Press referring to *Hints and Helps for Pressing Strip Sets* on page 152. Make a total of 10 strip sets. Cut strip sets into segments.

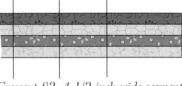

Crosscut 82, 4-1/2-inch wide segments

Step 7   Referring to quilt photograph, on page 90 for placement, sew together 19 of the segments, alternating the direction of the strips; press. <u>At this point pieced border should measure 4-1/2 x 76-1/2-inches.</u> Make a total of 2 pieced border strips for top/bottom edges. Sew border strips to top/bottom edges of quilt center; press.

Step 8   Referring to quilt photograph, on page 90 for placement, sew together 22 of the segments, alternating the direction of the strips; press. <u>At this point pieced border should measure 4-1/2 x 88-1/2-inches.</u> Make a total of 2 pieced border strips for side edges. Sew 4-1/2-inch black corner squares to both ends of each strip; press. Sew border strips to side edges of quilt center; press.

Step 9   Attach 8-1/2-inch wide **RED #2** outer border strips in the same manner as the **BLACK** inner border.

Putting It All Together

If using 108-inch wide backing fabric, simply trim backing and batting so they are 6-inches larger than quilt top. Refer to **Finishing the Quilt** on page 154 for complete instructions.

Note: If using 44-inch wide backing fabric, cut the 9 yard length of backing fabric in thirds crosswise to make 3, 3 yard lengths. Sew long edges together; press. Trim backing and batting so they are 6-inches larger than quilt top. Refer to **Finishing the Quilt** *on page 154 for complete instructions.*

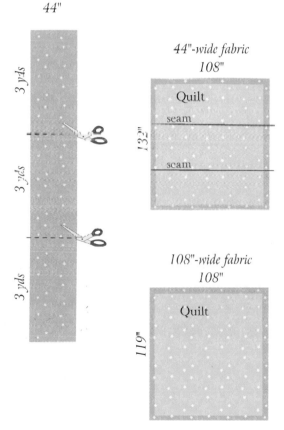

44"

3 yds

3 yds

3 yds

44"-wide fabric
108"

Quilt

seam

seam

132"

108"-wide fabric
108"

Quilt

119"

Finished Back Diagram

Quilting Suggestions:

- Houses in-the-ditch
- **BEIGE** backgrounds-stipple
- Trunks, doors, roofs, chimneys-channel stitch
- Star point-to-point
- **BROWN** rectangles-TB93—1-1/2" M-Border
- **BLACK** inner border-TB67—1-1/2" Heart Chain
- **RED** lattice-TB76—3-1/2" Holly Chain Border
- **RED** outer border-TB43—7" Star Vine Border

Thimbleberries® quilt stencils by Quilting Creations International are available at your local quilt shop or visit www.quiltingcreations.com.

Binding

Cutting

From **BROWN PRINT #2**:
- Cut 11, 2-3/4 x 44-inch strips

Sew binding to quilt using a 3/8-inch seam allowance. This measurement will produce a 1/2-inch wide finished double binding. Refer to **Binding** and **Diagonal Piecing** on page 154 for complete instructions.

HOMETOWN CHRISTMAS WALL QUILT

42 x 40-inches

Fabrics & Supplies

1/4 yard **DARK GOLD PRINT** for house block

3/4 yard **BEIGE FLORAL** for background

1/8 yard **BLACK PRINT** for house windows

1/8 yard **BROWN PRINT #1** for chimney, tree trunks

1/3 yard **BEIGE PRINT**
for tree background, hourglass blocks

1/3 yard **MEDIUM GREEN PRINT**
for tree blocks, wreath block

7/8 yard **DARK GREEN PRINT**
for tree blocks, outer border

1/4 yard **MEDIUM GOLD PRINT**
for hourglass blocks

1/8 yard **DARK BLUE PRINT** for pinwheel block

1/8 yard **LIGHT GREEN PRINT** for wreath block

3/8 yard **RED PRINT** for inner border

1/3 yard **BROWN PRINT #2** for dogtooth border

3/8 yard **RED PRINT** for binding

2-2/3 yards for backing fabric

quilt batting, at least 48 x 46-inches

Before beginning project, read through
Getting Started *on page 145.*

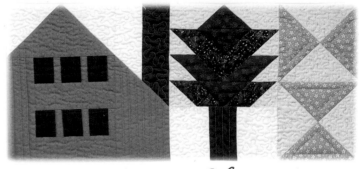

Hometown Christmas
House Block
Tree #1 Block
Hourglass Block

House Block

Make 1

Cutting

From **DARK GOLD PRINT**:
- Cut 1, 4-1/2 x 44-inch strip. From strip cut:
  2, 4-1/2 x 8-1/2-inch rectangles
  6, 1 x 2-1/2 inch rectangles
- Cut 1, 2-1/2 x 44-inch strip. From strip cut:
  1, 2-1/2 x 8-1/2-inch rectangle
  2, 2-1/2 x 6-1/2-inch rectangles

From **BEIGE FLORAL**:
- Cut 1, 4-1/2 x 22-inch strip. From strip cut:
  2, 4-1/2-inch squares
  1, 2-1/2 x 8-1/2-inch rectangle

From **BLACK PRINT**:
- Cut 1, 2 x 44-inch strip. From strip cut:
  6, 2 x 2-1/2-inch rectangles

From **BROWN PRINT #1**:
- Cut 1, 2-1/2 x 8-1/2-inch rectangle

Piecing

Step 1   Position a 4-1/2-inch **BEIGE FLORAL** square
on the corner of a 4-1/2 x 8-1/2-inch **DARK
GOLD** rectangle. Draw diagonal line on
square; stitch on line. Trim seam allowance to

1/4-inch; press. Repeat this process at opposite corner of rectangle to make roof unit.

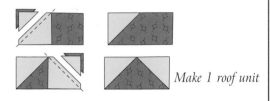

Make 1 roof unit

Step 2 Sew together 3 of the 1 x 2-1/2-inch **DARK GOLD** rectangles and 3 of the 2 x 2-1/2-inch **BLACK** rectangles; press. Make 2 window units. Sew together window units and 2-1/2 x 6-1/2-inch **DARK GOLD** rectangles; press. <u>At this point window unit should measure 6-1/2 x 8-1/2-inches.</u> Sew 2-1/2 x 8-1/2-inch **DARK GOLD** rectangle to left edge of window unit to make house unit; press. Sew roof unit to top edge of house unit; press. <u>At this point house unit should measure 8-1/2 x 12-inches.</u>

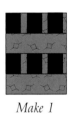

Make 2 window units

Make 1   *Make 1*

Step 3 Aligning long edges, sew together 2-1/2 x 8-1/2-inch **BEIGE FLORAL** and **BROWN #1** rectangles to make chimney unit; press. Position chimney unit on upper corner of 4-1/2 x 8-1/2-inch **DARK GOLD** rectangle. Draw diagonal line on chimney unit; stitch, trim, and press. <u>At this point unit should measure 4-1/2 x 12-1/2-inches.</u> Sew unit to right edge of house unit; press. <u>At this point house block should measure 12-1/2-inches square.</u>

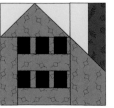

Make 1   *Make 1 house block*

Tree #1 Block

Make 1 Tree #1 block

Cutting

From **BEIGE PRINT**:
- Cut 1, 2-1/2 x 44-inch strip. From strip cut:
  2, 2-1/2 x 4-1/2-inch rectangles
  6, 2-1/2-inch squares

From **MEDIUM GREEN PRINT**:
- Cut 1, 2-1/2 x 44-inch strip. From strip cut:
  5, 2-1/2 x 4-1/2-inch rectangles

From **DARK GREEN PRINT**:
- Cut 1, 2-1/2 x 44-inch strip. From strip cut:
  5, 2-1/2 x 4-1/2-inch rectangles

From **BEIGE FLORAL**:
- Cut 2, 3-1/2 x 4-1/2-inch rectangles

From **BROWN PRINT #1**:
- Cut 1, 2-1/2 x 4-1/2-inch rectangle

Piecing

Step 1 Position a 2-1/2 x 4-1/2-inch **BEIGE PRINT** rectangle on the corner of a 2-1/2 x 4-1/2-inch **MEDIUM GREEN** rectangle; press. Draw diagonal line on **BEIGE PRINT** rectangle; stitch, trim, and press. Repeat this process at opposite corner of **MEDIUM GREEN** rectangle. <u>At this point the unit should measure 2-1/2 x 8-1/2-inches.</u>

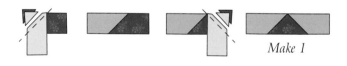

Make 1

Step 2 Position 2-1/2 x 4-1/2-inch **DARK GREEN** rectangle on the corner of a 2-1/2 x 4-1/2-inch **MEDIUM GREEN** rectangle; press. Draw diagonal line on **DARK GREEN** rectangle; stitch, trim, and press. Repeat this process at opposite corner of **MEDIUM GREEN** rectangle. Position 2-1/2-inch **BEIGE PRINT**

squares on the corners of the unit. Draw diagonal lines on squares; stitch, trim, and press. <u>At this point the unit should measure 2-1/2 x 8-1/2-inches.</u>

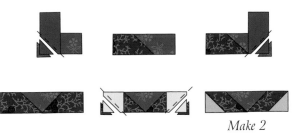

Make 2

Step 3   Position 2-1/2 x 4-1/2-inch **MEDIUM GREEN** rectangle on the corner of a 2-1/2 x 4-1/2-inch **DARK GREEN** rectangle; press. Draw diagonal line on **MEDIUM GREEN** rectangle; stitch, trim, and press. Repeat this process at opposite corner of **DARK GREEN** rectangle. Position 2-1/2-inch **BEIGE PRINT** squares on the corners of the unit. Draw diagonal lines on squares; stitch, trim, and press. <u>At this point the unit should measure 2-1/2 x 8-1/2-inches.</u>

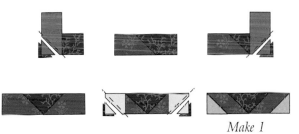

Make 1

Step 4   Sew 3-1/2 x 4-1/2-inch **BEIGE FLORAL** rectangles to both side edges of 2-1/2 x 4-1/2-inch **BROWN PRINT** rectangle; press.

Make 1

Step 5   Sew together Step 1, 2, 3, and 4 units; press. <u>At this point tree block should measure 8-1/2 x 12-1/2-inches.</u>

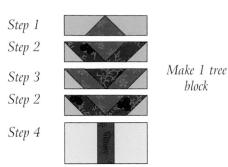

Step 1

Step 2

Step 3

Step 2   *Make 1 tree block*

Step 4

Step 6   Sew house and tree blocks together; press. <u>At this point house/tree section should measure 12-1/2 x 20-1/2-inches.</u>

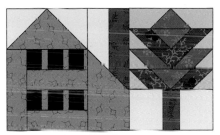

Make 1 house/tree section

Hourglass Block

Make 3 Hourglass blocks

Cutting

From **MEDIUM GOLD PRINT**:
  • Cut 1, 7-1/4 x 44-inch strip. From strip cut: 2, 7-1/4-inch squares

From **BEIGE PRINT**:
  • Cut 1, 7-1/4 x 44-inch strip. From strip cut: 2, 7-1/4-inch squares

Piecing

Step 1   With right sides together, layer 7-1/4-inch **MEDIUM GOLD** and **BEIGE PRINT** squares in pairs. Press together, but do not sew. Cut layered squares diagonally into quarters to make 8 sets of triangles. (You will be using only 6 sets of triangles.)

Step 2 Stitch along bias edge of each triangle set being careful not to stretch the triangles; press. Sew triangle units together in pairs; press. <u>At this point each hourglass block should measure 6-1/2-inches square.</u> Set hourglass blocks aside.

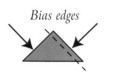

Bias edges

Make 6

Make 3

Step 3 Sew together 2 of the hourglass blocks; press. Sew this unit to right edge of house/tree unit; press. <u>At this point the section should measure 12-1/2 x 26-1/2-inches.</u>

Make 1

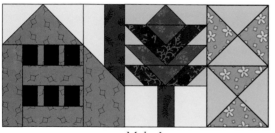

Make 1

Pinwheel Block

Make 1 block

Cutting

From **DARK BLUE PRINT**:
• Cut 2, 3-7/8-inch squares

From **BEIGE FLORAL**:
• Cut 2, 3-7/8-inch squares

Piecing

Step 1 With right sides together, layer 3-7/8-inch **DARK BLUE** and **BEIGE FLORAL** squares in pairs. Press together, but do not sew. Cut layered squares diagonally in half to make 4 sets of triangles. Stitch 1/4-inch from diagonal edge of each set of triangles; press.

 *Make 4, 3-1/2-inch triangle-pieced squares*

Step 2 Sew triangle-pieced squares together in pairs; press. Sew pairs together to make 1 pinwheel block. <u>At this point pinwheel block should measure 6-1/2-inches square.</u>

Make 2

Make 1

Step 3 Sew pinwheel block to bottom edge of remaining hourglass block; press. Set this unit aside.

Make 1

Hometown Christmas
Wreath Block
Tree #2 Block

Wreath Block

Make 1 block

Cutting

From **LIGHT GREEN PRINT**:
- Cut 1, 2-1/2 x 44-inch strip. From strip cut:
  12, 2-1/2-inch squares

From **BEIGE FLORAL**:
- Cut 1, 4-1/2 x 44-inch strip. From strip cut:
  1, 4-1/2-inch square
  8, 2-1/2 x 4-1/2-inch rectangles
  4, 2-1/2-inch squares

From **MEDIUM GREEN PRINT**:
- Cut 2, 2-1/2 x 44-inch strips. From strips cut:
  4, 2-1/2 x 4-1/2-inch rectangles
  12, 2-1/2-inch squares

Piecing

Step 1 Position 2-1/2-inch **LIGHT GREEN** squares on 2 opposite corners of the 4-1/2-inch **BEIGE FLORAL** square. Draw diagonal line on 2-1/2-inch squares; stitch, trim, and press. Repeat this process at the 2 opposite corners of the **BEIGE FLORAL** square; press.

Make 1

Step 2 Position a 2-1/2-inch **LIGHT GREEN** square on the corner of a 2-1/2 x 4-1/2-inch **MEDIUM GREEN** rectangle. Draw diagonal line on square; stitch, trim, and press. Repeat this process at opposite corner of rectangle; press.

Make 4

Step 3 Position a 2-1/2-inch **MEDIUM GREEN** square on the corner of 2-1/2 x 4-1/2-inch **BEIGE FLORAL** rectangle. Draw diagonal line on square; stitch, trim, and press. Repeat this process at opposite corner of rectangle; press. Make 4 units. Sew Step 2 units to bottom edge of the units; press.

Make 4

Make 4

Step 4 Sew Step 3 units to top/bottom edges of Step 1 unit; press.

Make 1

Step 5 Sew together 4 of the 2-1/2-inch **BEIGE FLORAL** and **MEDIUM GREEN** squares in pairs; press. Sew 2-1/2 x 4-1/2-inch **BEIGE FLORAL** rectangle to right edge of unit; press. Make 4 units.

Make 4

Step 6 Sew Step 5 units to edges of remaining Step 3 units; press. Sew these units to side edges of Step 4 unit; press. <u>At this point wreath block should measure 12-1/2-inches square.</u>

Make 1 wreath block

121

Tree #2 Block

Make 1 tree block

Cutting

From **DARK GREEN PRINT**:
- Cut 1, 4-7/8 x 22-inch strip. From strip cut:
  1, 4-7/8-inch square
  2, 2-1/2 x 4-1/2-inch rectangles
  2, 2-1/2-inch squares

From **BEIGE PRINT**:
- Cut 1, 4-7/8-inch square
- Cut 4, 2-1/2-inch squares

From **MEDIUM GREEN PRINT**:
- Cut 1, 2-1/2 x 22-inch strip. From strip cut:
  2, 2-1/2 x 4-1/2-inch rectangles
  4, 2-1/2-inch squares

From **BEIGE FLORAL**:
- Cut 2, 3-1/2 x 4-1/2-inch rectangles

From **BROWN PRINT #1**:
- Cut 1, 2-1/2 x 4-1/2-inch rectangle

Piecing

Step 1 With right sides together, layer 4-7/8-inch **DARK GREEN** and **BEIGE PRINT** squares. Press together, but do not sew. Cut layered square in half diagonally to make 2 sets of triangles. Stitch 1/4-inch from diagonal edge of each set of triangles.

Make 2, 4-1/2-inch triangle-pieced squares

Step 2 Position 2-1/2-inch **MEDIUM GREEN** squares on **DARK GREEN** corner of triangle-pieced squares. Draw diagonal line on **MEDIUM GREEN** squares; stitch, trim, and press. Make 2 units. Sew units together; press.

Make 2   *Make 1*

Step 3 Position a 2-1/2-inch **BEIGE PRINT** square on left corner of a 2-1/2 x 4-1/2-inch **MEDIUM GREEN** rectangle. Draw diagonal line on square; stitch, trim, and press. Repeat this process at opposite corner of rectangle using a 2-1/2-inch **DARK GREEN** square; press.

Make 1

Step 4 Position a 2-1/2-inch **DARK GREEN** square on left corner of a 2-1/2 x 4-1/2-inch **MEDIUM GREEN** rectangle. Draw diagonal line on square; stitch, trim, and press. Repeat this process at opposite corner of rectangle using a 2-1/2-inch **BEIGE** print square; press.

Make 1

Step 5 Sew together Step 3 and Step 4 units; press.

Make 1

Step 6 Position a 2-1/2-inch **BEIGE PRINT** square on left corner of a 2-1/2 x 4-1/2-inch **DARK GREEN** rectangle. Draw diagonal line on square; stitch, trim, and press. Repeat this process at opposite corner of rectangle using a 2-1/2-inch **MEDIUM GREEN** square.

Make 1

Step 7 Position 2-1/2-inch **MEDIUM GREEN** square on left corner of a 2-1/2 x 4-1/2-inch **DARK GREEN** rectangle. Draw diagonal line on square; stitch, trim, and press. Repeat this process at opposite corner of rectangle using a 2-1/2-inch **BEIGE PRINT** square.

Make 1

Step 8 Sew together Step 6 and Step 7 units; press.

Make 1

Step 9 Sew 3-1/2 x 4-1/2-inch **BEIGE FLORAL** rectangles to both side edges of 2-1/2 x 4-1/2-inch **BROWN #1** rectangle; press.

Make 1

Step 10 Sew together Step 2, Step 5, Step 8, and Step 9 units; press. <u>At this point tree block should measure 8-1/2 x 12-1/2-inches</u>.

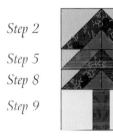

Step 2
Step 5   *Make 1 tree*
Step 8   *block*
Step 9

Step 11 Sew tree block and wreath block together; press. Sew pinwheel/ hourglass block to left edge of unit; press. <u>At this point pinwheel/hourglass/wreath/tree section should measure 12-1/2 x 26-1/2-inches</u>.

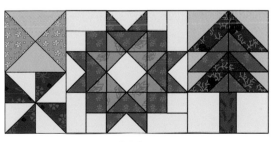

Make 1

Step 12 Referring to quilt center diagram, sew pinwheel/ hourglass/wreath/tree section to bottom edge of house/tree/hourglass section; press. <u>At this point quilt center should measure 26-1/2 x 24-1/2-inches</u>.

Quilt Center Diagram

Borders

*Note: Yardage given allows for border strips to be cut on crosswise grain. Read through **Borders** on page 153 for general instructions on adding borders.*

Cutting

From **RED PRINT**:
  • Cut 4, 2-1/2 x 44-inch inner border strips

From **BROWN PRINT #2**:
  • Cut 3, 2-7/8 x 44-inch strips.

From **BEIGE FLORAL**:
  • Cut 3, 2-7/8 x 44-inch strips.
  • Cut 4, 2-1/2-inch corner squares

From **DARK GREEN PRINT**:
  • Cut 4, 4-1/2 x 44-inch outer border strips

Attaching Border

Step 1 Attach 2-1/2-inch wide **RED** inner border.

Step 2 With right sides together layer 2-7/8 x 44-inch **BROWN #2** and **BEIGE FLORAL** strips in pairs. Press together, but do not sew. Cut layered strips into squares. Cut layered squares diagonally in half to make 58 sets of triangles. Stitch 1/4-inch from diagonal edge of each set of triangles; press.

Crosscut 29,
2-7/8-inch squares

Make 58,
2-1/2-inch triangle-
pieced squares

Step 3 For top/bottom sawtooth borders, sew together 15 triangle-pieced squares; press. Make 2 borders. Sew borders to quilt center; press.

Step 4 For side sawtooth borders, sew together 14 triangle-pieced squares; press. Make 2 borders. Sew 2-1/2-inch **BEIGE FLORAL** corner squares to both ends of border strips; press. Sew borders to quilt center; press.

Step 5 Attach 4-1/2-inch wide **DARK GREEN** outer border.

Putting It All Together

Cut 2-2/3 yard length of backing fabric in half crosswise to make 2, 1-1/3 yard lengths. Sew long edges together; press. Trim backing and batting so they are 6-inches larger than quilt top. Refer to *Finishing the Quilt* on page 154 for finishing instructions.

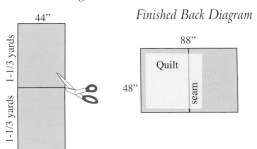

44"

1-1/3 yards

1-1/3 yards

Finished Back Diagram

88"

Quilt

48"

seam

Quilting Suggestions:

• All **BEIGE** background-stipple

• House block-channel stitch in house, meander in chimney

• Tree blocks-in-the-ditch on branches, channel stitch in trunks

• Wreath block-in-the-ditch

• **RED** inner border
   TB64—1-1/2" Nordic Scroll

Thimbleberries® quilt stencils by Quilting Creations International are available at your local quilt shop or visit www.quiltingcreations.com.

Binding

Cutting

From **RED** print:
   • Cut 4, 2-3/4 x 44-inch strips

Sew binding to quilt using a 3/8-inch seam allowance. This measurement will produce a 1/2-inch wide finished double binding. Refer to *Binding* and *Diagonal Piecing* on page 154 for complete instructions.

Hometown Christmas Wall Quilt
42 x 40-inches

December Dusk Runner

24 x 44-inches

Fabrics & Supplies

2/3 yard **MEDIUM GREEN PRINT** for blocks, sawtooth border, and corner squares

1/2 yard **BEIGE PRINT** for blocks and sawtooth border

1/4 yard **RED LEAF PRINT** for blocks

1/4 yard **RED/BROWN PRINT** for blocks

1/2 yard **BROWN PRINT** for outer border

3/8 yard **RED LEAF** print for binding

1-1/3 yards for backing fabric

quilt batting, at least 28 x 48-inches

Before beginning project, read through **Getting Started** *on page 145.*

December Dusk
Runner

Blocks

Makes 3 blocks

Cutting

From **MEDIUM GREEN PRINT**:
- Cut 1, 6-7/8 x 44-inch strip. From strip cut: 6, 6-7/8-inch squares
- Cut 1, 2-1/2 x 44-inch strip. From strip cut: 12, 2-1/2-inch squares

From **BEIGE PRINT**:
- Cut 2, 4-1/2 x 44-inch strips. From strips cut: 12, 4-1/2-inch squares

From **RED LEAF PRINT**:
- Cut 3, 6-7/8-inch squares

From **RED/BROWN PRINT**:
- Cut 3, 6-7/8-inch squares

Piecing

Step 1 With right sides together, layer 3 of the 6-7/8-inch **MEDIUM GREEN** squares and the 3 **RED LEAF** squares. Press together, but do not sew. Cut layered squares in half diagonally to make 6 sets of triangles. Stitch 1/4-inch from diagonal edge of each pair of triangles. Press seam allowance toward **RED** triangle.

Make 6, 6-1/2-inch triangle-pieced squares

Step 2 Layer a 4-1/2-inch **BEIGE** square on **MEDIUM GREEN** side of the triangle-pieced square. Draw diagonal line on **BEIGE** square; stitch on line. Trim seam allowance to 1/4 inch. Press seam allowance toward **MEDIUM GREEN** strip

Make 6

Step 3 Layer a 2-1/2-inch **MEDIUM GREEN** square on **BEIGE** side of the triangle-pieced square. Draw diagonal line on **MEDIUM GREEN** square; stitch and trim. Press seam allowance toward **BEIGE** strip. At this point each pieced square should measure 6-1/2-inches square.

Make 6

Step 4 With right sides together, layer 3 of the 6-7/8-inch **MEDIUM GREEN** squares and the 3 **RED/BROWN** squares. Press together, but do not sew. Cut layered squares in half diagonally to make 6 sets of triangles. Stitch 1/4-inch from diagonal edge of each pair of triangles. Press seam allowance toward **MEDIUM GREEN** triangle.

Make 6, 6-1/2-inch triangle-pieced squares

Step 5 Layer a 4-1/2-inch **BEIGE** square on **MEDIUM GREEN** side of the triangle-pieced square. Draw diagonal line on **BEIGE** square; stitch and trim. Press seam allowance toward **MEDIUM GREEN** strip.

Make 6

Step 6 Layer a 2-1/2-inch **MEDIUM GREEN** square on **BEIGE** side of the triangle-pieced square. Draw diagonal line on **MEDIUM GREEN** square; stitch and trim. Press seam allowance toward **MEDIUM GREEN** strip. At this point each pieced square should measure 6-1/2-inches square.

Make 6

Step 7 Referring to block diagram for color placement, sew pieced squares together to make 3 blocks; press. At this point each block should measure 12-1/2-inches square.

Make 3

Step 8 Referring to runner diagram for color placement, sew blocks together to make runner center. At this point runner center should measure 12-1/2 x 36-1/2-inches.

Sawtooth Border

Cutting

From **MEDIUM GREEN PRINT**:
• Cut 2, 2-7/8 x 44-inch strips.
  From 1 of the strips cut:
  2, 2-1/2 x 4-1/2-inch rectangles

From **BEIGE PRINT**:
• Cut 2, 2-7/8 x 44-inch strips.
  From 1 of the strips cut:
  4, 2-1/2-inch squares

Piecing

Step 1 With right sides together, layer 2-7/8 x 44-inch **MEDIUM GREEN** and **BEIGE** strips. Press together, but do not sew. Layer remaining strips in the same manner. Cut layered strips into squares. Cut squares in half diagonally to make 32 sets of triangles. Stitch 1/4-inch from diagonal edge of each pair of triangles; press.

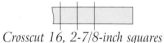

Crosscut 16, 2-7/8-inch squares

Make 32, 2-1/2-inch triangle-pieced squares

Step 2 Sew together 8 of the triangle-pieced squares; press. Make 2 sawtooth units. Sew together 8 more triangle-pieced squares, note the direction of the seam lines; press. Make 2 sawtooth units.

Make 2 sawtooth units

Make 2 sawtooth units

Step 3 Position a 2-1/2-inch **BEIGE** square on the corner of a 2-1/2 x 4-1/2-inch **MEDIUM GREEN** rectangle. Draw diagonal line on square; stitch, trim, and press. Repeat this process at opposite corner of rectangle.

Make 2

Step 4 Sew Step 2 sawtooth units to both side edges of the Step 3 units; press. Sew sawtooth borders to long side edges of runner center; press.

Make 2

Border

Note: Yardage given allows for border strips to be cut on crosswise grain.

Cutting

From **MEDIUM GREEN PRINT**:
- Cut 4, 4-1/2-inch corner squares

From **BROWN PRINT**:
- Cut 3, 4-1/2 x 44-inch outer border strips

Attaching Border

Step 1 With pins, mark center points along all 4 sides of runner. For top/bottom borders measure runner from left to right through the middle.

Step 2 Measure and mark border lengths and center points on the 4-1/2-inch wide **BROWN PRINT** strips cut for borders before sewing them on.

Step 3 Pin border strips to runner matching the pinned points on each of the borders and the runner. Stitch a 1/4-inch seam; press. Trim off excess border lengths.

Step 4 For side outer borders, measure runner top including seam allowances, but not top/bottom borders. Cut the 4-1/2-inch wide **BROWN PRINT** side outer border strips to this length. Sew 4 1/2-inch **MEDIUM GREEN** corner square to both ends of the border strips; press. Sew border strips to side edges of runner center; press.

Putting It All Together

Trim backing and batting so they are 4-inches larger than runner top. Mark runner top for quilting. Layer backing, batting, and runner top. Baste the 3 layers together and quilt. Refer to *Finishing the Quilt* on page 154 for finishing instructions.

Quilting Suggestions:

- **GREEN/BEIGE** pieced blocks
  TB 85—7-1/2" Heart Swirl

- **RED** pieced side triangles-TB 49—9" Corner Hearts

- **RED** corner triangles-TB 49—7" Corner Hearts

- **BEIGE** sawtooth border-stipple

- **BROWN** outer border
  TB 48—3-1/2" Border Heart

- **GREEN** corner squares
  TB 51—3-1/2" Oak Leaf

Thimbleberries® *quilt stencils by Quilting Creations International are available at your local quilt shop or visit www.quiltingcreations.com.*

Binding

Cutting

From **RED LEAF PRINT**:
- Cut 4, 2-3/4 x 44-inch strips

Sew binding to quilt using a 3/8-inch seam allowance. This measurement will produce a 1/2-inch wide finished double binding. Refer to *Binding* and *Diagonal Piecing* on page 154 for complete instructions.

December Dusk Runner
24 x 44-inches

GIFT PACKAGE PILLOW SHAM

20 x 28-inches

Fabrics & Supplies

Note: *Fabrics and Supplies are for 1 pillow sham*

1/8 yard **DARK GOLD PRINT** for bow

1/4 yard **MEDIUM GOLD PRINT** for bow

1-5/8 yards **BEIGE PRINT**
for background, borders, pillow back

1/4 yard **DARK GREEN PRINT** for package

1/4 yard **RED PRINT** for package

1/4 yard **BROWN PRINT** for package

1/4 yard **MEDIUM GREEN PRINT** for package

1/3 yard **DARK GREEN PRINT** for binding

25 x 33-inch muslin rectangle for pillow top lining

quilt batting, at least 25 x 33-inches

20 x 28-inch pillow form

Before beginning project, read through
Getting Started *on page 145.*

Pillow Top

Cutting

From **DARK GOLD PRINT**:
- Cut 1, 3-1/2 x 44-inch strip. From strip cut:
  16, 1-1/2 x 3-1/2-inch rectangles
  4, 1-1/2-inch squares

From **MEDIUM GOLD PRINT**:
- Cut 1, 5-1/2 x 44-inch strip. From strip cut:
  8, 1-1/2 x 5-1/2-inch rectangles
  4, 1-1/2 x 4-1/2-inch rectangles

From **BEIGE PRINT**:
- Cut 3, 1-1/2 x 44-inch strips. From strips cut:
  8, 1-1/2 x 4-1/2-inch rectangles
  8, 1-1/2 x 3-1/2-inch rectangles
  8, 1-1/2 x 2-inch rectangles
  8, 1-1/2-inch squares

From **DARK GREEN PRINT, RED PRINT,
BROWN PRINT, MEDIUM GREEN PRINT**:
- Cut 1, 3-1/2 x 44-inch strip. From strip cut:
  2, 3-1/2 x 4-1/2-inch rectangles
  2, 1-1/2 x 2-1/2-inch rectangles
  2, 1-1/2-inch squares

Piecing the Packages

Step 1 Position a 1-1/2 x 3-1/2-inch **BEIGE** rectangle on left corner of 1-1/2 x 3-1/2-inch **DARK GOLD** rectangle. Draw diagonal line on **BEIGE** rectangle; stitch, trim, and press. Position a 1-1/2 x 2-inch **BEIGE** rectangle on right corner of **DARK GOLD** rectangle. Draw diagonal line on **BEIGE** rectangle; stitch, trim, and press. <u>At this point each unit should measure 1-1/2 x 6-inches.</u>

Make 4

Step 2 Position a 1-1/2 x 2-inch **BEIGE** rectangle on left corner of 1-1/2 x 3-1/2-inch **DARK GOLD** rectangle. Draw diagonal line on **BEIGE** rectangle; stitch, trim, and press. Position a 1-1/2 x 3-1/2-inch **BEIGE** rectangle on right corner of **DARK GOLD** rectangle. Draw diagonal line on **BEIGE** rectangle; stitch, trim, and press. <u>At this point each unit should measure 1-1/2 x 6-inches.</u>

Make 4

Step 3 Sew together Step 1 and Step 2 units in pairs; press. <u>At this point each unit should measure 1-1/2 x 11-1/2-inches.</u>

Step 1   Step 2
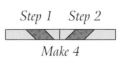
Make 4

Step 4 Position a 1-1/2-inch **BEIGE** square on left corner of a 1-1/2 x 5-1/2-inch **MEDIUM GOLD** rectangle. Draw diagonal line on square; stitch, trim, and press. Make 8 units. Sew units to both side edges of a 1-1/2-inch **DARK GOLD** square; press. At this point each unit should measure 1-1/2 x 11-1/2-inches.

Make 8   *Make 4*

Step 5   Sew together Step 3 and Step 4 units in pairs; press. At this point each bow unit should measure 2-1/2 x 11-1/2-inches.

Step 3
Step 4   *Make 4 bow units*

Step 6   To make **DARK GREEN** package, position a 1-1/2 x 2-1/2-inch **DARK GREEN** rectangle on left corner of 1-1/2 x 3-1/2-inch **DARK GOLD** rectangle. Draw diagonal line on **DARK GREEN** rectangle; stitch, trim, and press. Repeat this process at right corner of **DARK GOLD** rectangle using a 1-1/2-inch **DARK GREEN** square. Sew a 3-1/2 x 4-1/2-inch **DARK GREEN** rectangle to bottom edge of unit; press. At this point unit should measure 4-1/2-inches square.

Make 1   *Make 1*

Step 7   Position a 1-1/2-inch **DARK GREEN** square on left corner of 1-1/2 x 3-1/2-inch **DARK GOLD** rectangle. Draw diagonal line on **DARK GREEN** square; stitch, trim, and press. Repeat this process at right corner of **DARK GOLD** rectangle using 1-1/2 x 2-1/2-inch **DARK GREEN** rectangle. Sew a 3-1/2 x 4-1/2-inch **DARK GREEN** rectangle to bottom edge of unit; press. At this point unit should measure 4-1/2-inches square.

Make 1   *Make 1*

Step 8   Sew together Step 6 unit, Step 7 unit, 1 of the 1-1/2 x 4-1/2-inch **MEDIUM GOLD** rectangles, and 2 of the 1-1/2 x 4-1/2-inch **BEIGE** rectangles; press. Sew a Step 5 bow

unit to top edge of package unit; press. At this point **DARK GREEN** package unit should measure 6-1/2 x 11-1/2-inches.

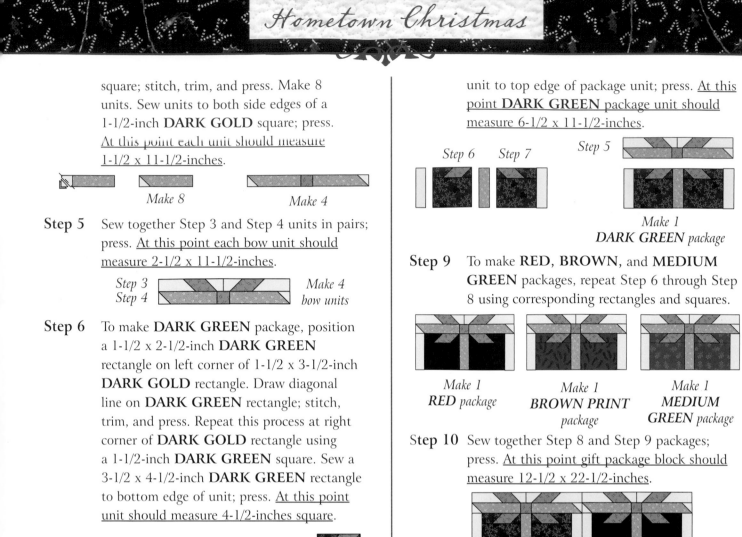

Make 1 DARK GREEN package

Step 9   To make **RED**, **BROWN**, and **MEDIUM GREEN** packages, repeat Step 6 through Step 8 using corresponding rectangles and squares.

Make 1 RED package   *Make 1 BROWN PRINT package*   *Make 1 MEDIUM GREEN package*

Step 10   Sew together Step 8 and Step 9 packages; press. At this point gift package block should measure 12-1/2 x 22-1/2-inches.

Make 1 gift package block

Border

*Note: Yardage given allows for border strips to be cut on crosswise grain. Read through **Border** instructions on page 153 for general instructions on adding borders.*

Cutting

From **BEIGE PRINT**:
- Cut 2, 4-3/4 x 44-inch top/bottom border strips
- Cut 1, 3-3/4 x 44-inch side border strip

Attaching Border

Step 1   Attach 4-3/4-inch wide **BEIGE** top/bottom border strips.

Step 2   Attach 3-3/4-inch wide **BEIGE** side border strips.

Quilt the Pillow Top

Cutting

From **MUSLIN AND BATTING**:
- Cut 1, 25 x 32-inch rectangle from each

Quilting

Step 1   Layer the muslin rectangle, batting rectangle, and pieced pillow top with right sides facing up. Hand baste layers together.

Step 2   Quilt pillow top. Our sample was quilted with crosshatching behind the gift packages and a feather design in the border. The packages are quilted in-the-ditch.

Step 3   When quilting is complete, trim pillow top to 20-3/4 x 28-3/4-inches. Hand baste edges together to prevent them from rippling when binding is attached.

Pillow Back

Cutting

From **BEIGE PRINT**:
- Cut 2, 20-3/4 x 36-inch pillow back rectangles

Pillow Back Assembly

Step 1   With wrong sides together, fold each 20-3/4 x 36-inch pillow back rectangle in half

crosswise to make 2, 18 x 20-3/4-inch double-thick pillow back pieces. Overlap 2 folded edges so pillow back measures 20-3/4 x 28-3/4-inches. Pin pieces together and stitch around entire piece to create a single pillow back, using a scant 1/4-inch seam allowance. The double thickness of each back piece will make pillow back more stable and give it a nice finishing touch.

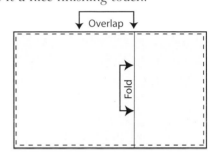

Step 2   With <u>wrong sides</u> together, layer pillow back and pillow top. Pin and stitch around outside edges using a 1/4-inch seam allowance.

Binding

Cutting

From **DARK GREEN PRINT**:
- Cut 3, 2-3/4 x 44-inch strips.

Attach binding using a 3/8-inch seam allowance. Refer to **Binding** and **Diagonal Piecing** instructions on page 154 for complete instructions.

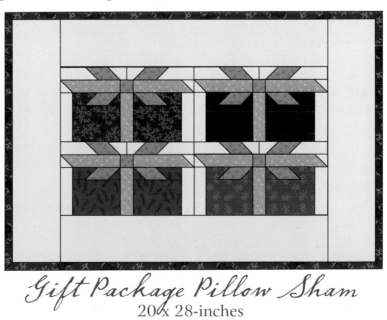

Gift Package Pillow Sham
20 x 28-inches

CORNER FLOWER PILLOW

20-inch square pillow without ruffle

Fabrics & Supplies

1/8 yard **DARK BLUE PRINT** for flowers

5 x 12-inch piece **RED PRINT** for flower centers

1/4 yard **BEIGE PRINT** for background

1/8 yard **LIGHT GREEN PRINT**
for leaves, center square

1/4 yard **GOLD PRINT** for inner border

1-3/8 yards **DARK GREEN PRINT**
for outer border, ruffle

7/8 yard **GREEN PRINT** for pillow backing fabric

24-inch muslin square for pillow top

quilt batting, at least 24-inches square

20-inch square pillow form

Before beginning this project, read through
Getting Started *on page 145.*

Corner Flower Pillow

Flower Block

Cutting

From **DARK BLUE PRINT**:
- Cut 2, 1-1/2 x 44-inch strips. From strips cut:
  8, 1-1/2 x 2-1/2-inch rectangles
  16, 1-1/2-inch squares

From **RED PRINT**:
- Cut 4, 2-1/2-inch squares

From **BEIGE PRINT**:
- Cut 1, 2-1/2 x 44-inch strip. From strip cut:
  4, 2-1/2 x 5-1/2-inch rectangles
  4, 2-1/2-inch squares
- Cut 1, 1-1/2 x 44-inch strip. From strip cut:
  16, 1-1/2 x 2-1/2-inch rectangles

From **LIGHT GREEN PRINT**:
- Cut 1, 2-1/2-inch center square
- Cut 1, 1-1/2 x 34-inch strip. From strip cut:
  4, 1-1/2 x 4-1/2-inch rectangles
  4, 1-1/2 x 3-1/2-inch rectangles

Piecing

Step 1 Position a 1-1/2-inch **DARK BLUE** square
on the corner of a 1-1/2 x 2-1/2-inch **BEIGE**
rectangle. Draw diagonal line on square;
stitch on line. Trim seam allowance to
1/4-inch; press. Repeat this process at
opposite corner of rectangle. Make 8 units.
Sew 1-1/2 x 2-1/2-inch **DARK BLUE**
rectangles to bottom edge of each unit;
press. At this point each unit should measure
2-1/2-inches square.

Make 8

Make 8

Step 2 Referring to diagram for placement, sew
together 2-1/2-inch **BEIGE** square, 2-1/2-inch
RED square, and 2 of the Step 1 units; press.
At this point each flower unit should measure
4-1/2-inches square.

Make 4 flower units

Step 3 Position a 1-1/2 x 2-1/2-inch **BEIGE** rectangle on left corner of a 1-1/2 x 3-1/2-inch **LIGHT GREEN** rectangle. Draw diagonal line on **BEIGE** rectangle; stitch, trim; press. Make 4 leaf units. Sew leaf units to left edge of flower units; press.

Make 4

Make 4

Step 4 Position a 1-1/2 x 2-1/2-inch **BEIGE** rectangle on right corner of a 1-1/2 x 4-1/2-inch **LIGHT GREEN** rectangle. Draw diagonal line on **BEIGE** rectangle; stitch, trim; press. Make 4 leaf units. Sew leaf units to bottom edge of flower units; press. <u>At this point each flower unit should measure 5-1/2-inches square.</u>

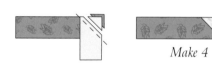

Make 4

Make 4

Step 5 Sew 2 of the flower units to both side edges of a 2-1/2 x 5-1/2-inch **BEIGE** rectangle; press. Make 2 units. Sew 2-1/2 x 5-1/2-inch **BEIGE** rectangles to both side edges of the 2-1/2-inch **LIGHT GREEN** center square; press. Sew units together to make flower block; press. <u>At this point flower block should measure 12-1/2-inches square.</u>

Make 1 flower block

Borders

*Note: Yardage given allows for border strips to be cut on crosswise grain. Read through **Border** instructions on page 153 for general instructions on adding borders.*

Cutting

From **GOLD PRINT**:
• Cut 2, 2-1/2 x 44-inch inner border strips

From **DARK GREEN PRINT**:
• Cut 2, 2-1/2 x 44-inch outer border strips

Attaching Borders

Step 1 Attach 2-1/2-inch wide **GOLD PRINT** inner border strips.

Step 2 Attach 2-1/2-inch wide **DARK GREEN PRINT** outer border strips.

Pillow Assembly

Step 1 Layer 24-inch muslin lining square, batting square, and pieced pillow top. Hand baste layers together; quilt as desired. When quilting is complete, trim excess batting and backing even with pillow top.

Quilting Suggestions:

• Flower blocks-in-the-ditch

• **BEIGE** background-stipple

• **GOLD** inner border
  TB67—1-1/2" Heart Chain

• **DARK GREEN** outer border-meander

Thimbleberries® quilt stencils by Quilting Creations International are available at your local quilt shop or visit www.quiltingcreations.com.

Step 2 To prepare pillow top before attaching ruffle, hand baste edges together. This will prevent the edge of the pillow top from rippling when attaching ruffle.

Pillow Ruffle

Cutting

From **DARK GREEN PRINT**:
• Cut 6, 6-3/4 x 44-inch strips

Attaching Ruffle

Step 1 Diagonally piece 6-3/4-inch wide **DARK GREEN** strips together to make a continuous ruffle strip. Fold strip in half lengthwise, wrong sides together; press. Divide ruffle strip into 4 equal segments; mark quarter points with safety pins.

Step 2 To gather ruffle, position a heavy thread 1/4-inch in from raw edges of ruffle strip. You will need a length of thread 200-inches long. Secure one end of the thread by stitching across it. Zigzag stitch over the thread all the way around ruffle strip taking care not to sew through it.

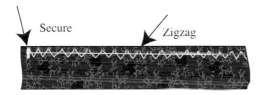

Secure · Zigzag

Step 3 Divide edges of pillow front into 4 equal segments and mark quarter points with safety pins. With right sides together and raw edges aligned, pin ruffle to pillow top, matching quarter points. Pull up gathering stitches until ruffle fits pillow front, taking care to allow extra fullness in ruffle at each corner. Sew ruffle to pillow front, using a 1/4-inch seam allowance.

Pillow Back

Cutting

From **GREEN PRINT**:
• Cut 2, 20-1/2 x 27-inch pillow back rectangles

Assembling Pillow Back

Step 1 With wrong sides together, fold each 20-1/2 x 27-inch **GREEN** rectangle in half to make 2, 13-1/2 x 20-1/2-inch double-thick pillow back pieces. Overlap the 2 folded edges so pillow back measures 20-1/2-inches square.

Pin pieces together and stitch around entire piece, using a scant 1/4-inch seam allowance, to create a single pillow back.

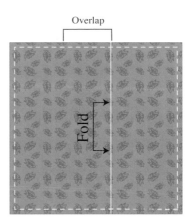

Overlap

Fold

Step 2 With right sides together, layer pillow back and pillow top; pin. The ruffle will be sandwiched between the 2 layers and turned toward center of pillow at this time. Pin and stitch around outside edges using a 1/2-inch seam allowance.

Step 3 Turn pillow right side out, insert pillow form through pillow back opening, and fluff up ruffle.

Corner Flower Pillow
20-inches square without ruffle

QUILTED PILLOW SHAM
20 x 29-inches

Fabrics & Supplies

Note: Fabrics and Supplies are for 1 pillow sham

1-3/4 yards **RED PRINT** for pillow top and back

1-1/8 yards **BROWN PRINT** for ruffle

24 x 33-inch muslin rectangle for pillow top lining

quilt batting, at least 24 x 33-inches

20 x 29-inch pillow form

Before beginning project, read through **Getting Started** *on page 145.*

Cutting

From **RED PRINT**:
• Cut 1, 24 x 33-inch pillow top rectangle

From muslin lining and quilt batting:
• Cut 1, 24 x 33-inch rectangle of each

Quilt the Pillow Top

Step 1 Layer the 24 x 33-inch **RED** rectangle, quilt batting rectangle, and muslin lining rectangle with right sides facing out. Pin or hand baste layers together.

Step 2 Quilt pillow top with a meander design. When quilting is complete, trim pillow top to 21 x 30-inches. To prepare pillow top before attaching ruffle, hand baste layers together. This will prevent edges of pillow top from rippling when ruffle is attached.

Pillow Ruffle

Cutting

From **BROWN PRINT**:
• Cut 6, 6-1/2 x 44-inch strips

Attaching Ruffle

Step 1 Diagonally piece ruffle strips together to make a continuous ruffle strip. Fold strip in half lengthwise, wrong sides together; press. Divide ruffle strip into 4 equal segments; mark quarter points with safety pins.

Step 2 To gather ruffle, position quilting thread 1/4-inch from raw edges of folded ruffle strip. You will need a length of thread 200-inches long. Secure one end of thread by stitching across it. Zigzag stitch over thread all the way around ruffle strip, taking care not to sew through it.

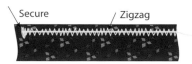

Step 3 Divide edges of pillow top into 4 equal segments; mark quarter points with safety pins. With right sides together and raw edges aligned, pin ruffle to pillow top, matching quarter points. Pull up gathering stitches until ruffle fits pillow top, taking care to allow extra fullness in the ruffle at each corner. Sew ruffle to pillow front using a 1/4-inch seam allowance

Pillow Back

Cutting

From **RED PRINT**:
• Cut 2, 21 x 36-inch pillow back rectangles

Pillow Back Assembly

Step 1 With wrong sides together, fold each 21 x 36-inch **RED** pillow back rectangle in half crosswise to make 2, 18 x 21-inch double-thick pillow back pieces. Overlap 2 folded edges so pillow back measures 21 x 30-inches. Pin pieces together and stitch

around entire piece to create a single pillow back, using a scant 1/4-inch seam allowance. The double thickness of each back piece will make pillow back more stable and give it a nice finishing touch.

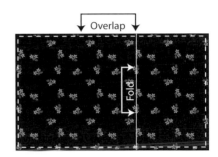

Step 2 With right sides together, layer pillow back and pillow top; pin. The ruffle will be sandwiched between the 2 layers and turned toward the center of pillow at this time. Pin and stitch around outside edges using a 1/2-inch seam allowance.

Step 3 Turn pillow right side out, insert pillow form through back opening, and fluff up ruffle.

HOMETOWN TABLE TOPPER AND MINI TREE SKIRT

30-inches square

Fabrics & Supplies

5/8 yard **GOLD PRINT** for star center, binding

1/2 yard **RED PRINT** for star points, middle borders

1/3 yard **BEIGE PRINT** for star background

1/4 yard **GREEN PRINT** for inner border

1/2 yard **GREEN/RED PRINT**
for middle border, outer border

1 yard for backing fabric

quilt batting, at least 36-inches square

Before beginning project, read through
Getting Started *on page 145.*

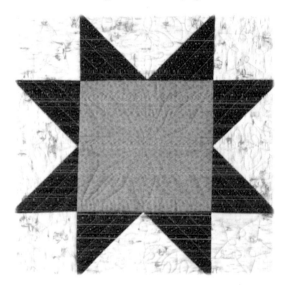

Hometown Table Topper
Star Block

Cutting

From **GOLD PRINT**:
- Cut 4, 2-3/4 x 44-inch strips to bind the straight edges (set strips aside to be used for binding)
- Cut 1, 8-1/2-inch square

From **RED PRINT**:
- Cut 1, 4-1/2 x 44-inch strip. From strip cut:
  8, 4-1/2-inch squares

From **BEIGE PRINT**:
- Cut 2, 4-1/2 x 44-inch strips. From strips cut:
  4, 4-1/2 x 8-1/2-inch rectangles
  4, 4-1/2-inch squares

Piecing

Step 1 Position a 4-1/2-inch **RED** square on the corner of a 4-1/2 x 8-1/2-inch **BEIGE** rectangle. Draw diagonal line on square; stitch on line. Trim seam allowance to 1/4-inch; press. Repeat this process at opposite corner of rectangle.

*Make 4 star
point units*

Step 2 Sew Step 1 star point units to top/bottom edges of 8-1/2-inch **GOLD** square; press. Sew 4-1/2-inch **BEIGE** squares to both ends of remaining star point units; press. Sew the units to side edges of **GOLD** square unit; press. At this point star block should measure 16-1/2-inches square.

Make 1 star block

Borders

Note: *The yardage given allows for the border strips to be cut on the crosswise grain. Diagonally piece the strips as needed, referring to **Diagonal Piecing** on page 154. Read through **Borders** on page 153 for general instructions on adding borders.*

Cutting

From **GREEN PRINT**:
- Cut 2, 2-1/2 x 44-inch inner border strips

From **RED PRINT**:
- Cut 7, 1-1/2 x 44-inch middle border strips

From **GREEN/RED PRINT**:
- Cut 4, 2-1/2 x 44-inch outer border strips
- Cut 4, 1-1/2 x 44-inch middle border strips

Attaching Borders

Step 1 Attach 2-1/2-inch wide **GREEN** inner border strips.

Step 2 Attach 1-1/2-inch wide **RED** middle border strips.

Step 3 Attach 1-1/2-inch wide **GREEN/ RED** middle border strips.

Step 4 Attach 1-1/2-inch wide **RED** middle border strips.

Step 5 Attach 2-1/2-inch wide **GREEN/ RED** outer border strips.

Putting It All Together

Trim backing and batting so they are 6-inches larger than quilt top. Layer backing, batting, and quilt top. Baste the 3 layers together and quilt as desired. Refer to *Finishing the Quilt* on page 145 for finishing instructions.

Quilting Suggestions:

• **GOLD** center square-TB46—7-1/2" Leaf Bouquet

• **RED** star points-echo

• **BEIGE** triangles-1/2 of **TB17—5"** Lady Slipper

• **BEIGE** squares-star only from **TB45—5"** Star Heart

• 5 borders quilted as 1 border
   TB69—5-1/2" Heart Chain (hearts turned)

Thimbleberries® *quilt stencils by Quilting Creations International are available at your local quilt shop or visit www.quiltingcreations.com.*

Binding the Quilt

Cutting

From **GOLD PRINT**:
   • The 4, 2-3/4 x 44-inch binding strips were cut previously in **Star Block** section.

Sew binding to quilt using a 3/8-inch seam allowance. This measurement will produce a 1/2-inch wide finished double binding. Refer to *Binding* and *Diagonal Piecing* on page 154 for complete instructions.

Binding the Tree Skirt

From **GOLD PRINT**:
   • The 4, 2-3/4 x 44-inch binding strips were cut previously in **Star Block** section.
   • Cut enough 2-1/2-inch wide **bias** strips to make a 44-inch long strip for center binding and ties

Attaching Binding and Ties

Step 1 To transform quilt into a tree skirt, use **Center Circle** template on page 143 to draw a circle at center of quilt. Draw a straight line from circle to midpoint of one edge of the quilt.

Step 2 Machine stitch a scant 1/4-inch outside the circle and a scant 1/4-inch away from both sides of straight line. Referring to diagram, cut through quilt top, batting, and backing on the straight line and on the drawn circle.

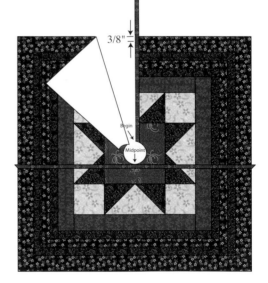

Step 3 Diagonally piece 2-3/4-inch wide **GOLD** binding strips. Fold strip in half lengthwise, wrong sides together; press.

Step 4 With raw edges even and using a 3/8-inch seam allowance, stitch the 2-3/4-inch wide **GOLD** binding strip to the tree skirt. Referring to diagram above, begin and end at inner corner of straight edge and center circle.

Step 5 Miter binding at corners. As you approach quilt corner, stop sewing 3/8-inch from the corner. Clip threads and remove tree skirt from

Squaring Up Blocks

To square up your blocks, first check the seam allowances. This is usually where the problem is, and it is always best to alter within the block rather than trim the outer edges. Next, make sure you have pressed accurately. Sometimes a block can become distorted by ironing instead of pressing.

To trim up block edges, use one of the many clear acrylic squares available on the market. Determine the center of the block; mark with a pin. Lay the square over the block and align as many perpendicular and horizontal lines as you can to the seams in your block. This will indicate where the block is off.

Do not trim all off on one side; this usually results in real distortion of the pieces in the block and the block design. Take a little fabric off all sides until the block is square. When assembling many blocks, it is necessary to make sure all are the same size.

Tools and Equipment

Making beautiful quilts does not require a large number of specialized tools or expensive equipment. My list of favorites is short and sweet and includes the things I use over and over again because they are always accurate and dependable.

I find a long acrylic ruler indispensable for accurate rotary cutting. The ones I like most are an Omnigrid® 6 x 24-inch grid acrylic ruler for cutting long strips and squaring up fabrics and quilt tops and a MasterPiece® 45-degree (8 x 24-inch) ruler for cutting 6- to 8-inch wide borders. I sometimes tape together two 6 x 24-inch acrylic rulers for cutting borders up to 12-inches wide.

A 15-inch Omnigrid® square acrylic ruler is great for squaring up individual blocks and corners of a quilt top, for cutting strips up to 15-inches wide or long, and for trimming side and corner triangles.

I think the markings on my 24 x 36-inch Olfa® rotary cutting mat stay visible longer than on other mats, and the lines are fine and accurate.

The largest size Olfa® rotary cutter cuts through many layers of fabric easily, and isn't cumbersome to use. The 2-1/2-inch blade slices through three layers of backing, batting, and a quilt top like butter.

An 8-inch pair of Gingher shears is great for cutting out appliqué templates and cutting fabric from a bolt or fabric scraps.

I keep a pair of 5-1/2-inch Gingher scissors by my sewing machine so it is handy for both machine work and handwork. This size is versatile and sharp enough to make large and small cuts equally well.

My Grabbit® magnetic pincushion has a surface that is large enough to hold lots of straight pins and a magnet strong enough to keep them securely in place.

Silk pins are long and thin, which means they won't leave large holes in your fabric. I like them because they increase accuracy in pinning pieces or blocks together. It is also easy to press over silk pins.

For pressing individual pieces, blocks, and quilt tops, I use an 18 x 48-inch sheet of plywood covered with several layers of cotton fiberfill and topped with a layer of muslin stapled to the back. The 48-inch length allows me to press an entire width of fabric at one time without the need to reposition it, and the square ends are better than tapered ends on an ironing board for pressing finished quilt tops.

Using Grain

The fabric you purchase still has selvage and before beginning to handle or cut your fabric, it's helpful to be able to recognize and understand its basic characteristics. Fabric is produced in the mill with identifiable grain or direction. These are: lengthwise, crosswise, and bias.

The lengthwise grain is the direction that fabric comes off the milling machine, and is parallel to the selvage. This grain of the fabric has the least stretch and the greatest strength.

The crosswise grain is the short distance that spans a bolt's 42-inch to 44-inch width. The crosswise grain, or width of grain, is between two sides called selvages. This grain of the fabric has medium stretch and medium strength.

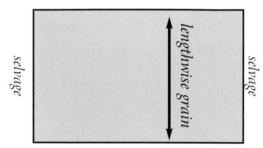

Most strength and least stretch

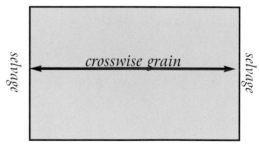

Medium strength and medium stretch

Avoiding Bias

The 45-degree angle on a piece of fabric is the bias and the direction with the most stretch. I suggest avoiding sewing on the bias until you're confident handling fabric. With practice and careful handling, bias edges can be sewn and are best for making curves.

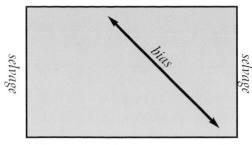

Least strength and most stretch

Rotary Cutting

SAFETY FIRST! The blades of a rotary cutter are very sharp and need to be for accurate cutting. Look at a variety of cutters to find one that feels good in your hand. All quality cutters have a safety mechanism to "close" the cutting blade when not in use. After each cut and before laying the rotary cutter down, close the blade. Soon this will become second nature to you and will prevent dangerous accidents. Always keep cutters out of the sight of children. Rotary cutters are very tempting to fiddle with when they are laying around. When your blade is dull or nicked, change it. Damaged blades do not cut accurately and require extra effort that can also result in slipping and injury. Also, always cut away from yourself for safety.

Squaring Off Fabric

Fold the fabric in half lengthwise matching the selvage edges.

Square off the ends of your fabric before measuring and cutting pieces. This means that the cut edge of the fabric must be exactly perpendicular to the folded edge which creates a 90-degree angle. Align the folded and selvage edges of the fabric with the lines on the cutting board, and place a ruled square on the fold. Place a 6 x 24-inch ruler against the side of the square to get a 90-degree angle. Hold the ruler in place, remove the square, and cut along the edge of the ruler. If you are left-handed, work from the other end of the fabric. Use the lines on your cutting board to help line up fabric, but not to measure and cut strips. Use a ruler for accurate cutting, always checking to make sure your fabric is lined up with horizontal and vertical lines on the ruler.

6 x 24" ruler

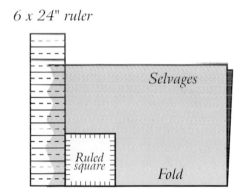

Cutting Strips

When cutting strips or rectangles, cut on the crosswise grain. Strips can then be cut into squares or smaller rectangles.

If your strips are not straight after cutting a few of them, refold the fabric, align the folded and selvage edges with the lines on the cutting board, and "square off" the edge again by trimming to straighten, and begin cutting.

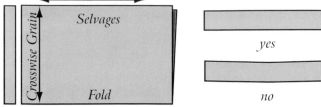

Lengthwise Grain

Selvages

Crosswise Grain

Fold

yes

no

Cutting Bias Strips

When cutting bias strips, trim your yardage on the crosswise grain so the edges are straight. With right sides facing up, fold the yardage on the diagonal. Fold the selvage edge (lengthwise grain) over to meet the cut edge (crosswise grain), forming a triangle. This diagonal fold is the true bias. Position the ruler to the desired strip width from the cut edge and cut one strip. Continue moving the ruler across the fabric cutting parallel strips in the desired widths.

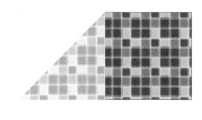

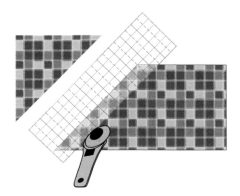

Trimming Side and Corner Triangles

In projects with side and corner triangles, the instructions have you cut side and corner triangles larger than needed. This will allow you to square up the quilt and eliminates the frustration of ending up with pre-cut side and corner triangles that don't match the size of your pieced blocks.

To cut triangles, first cut squares. The project directions will tell you what size to make the squares and whether to cut them in half to make two triangles or to cut them in quarters to make four triangles, as shown in the diagrams. This cutting method will give you side triangles that have the straight grain on the outside edges of the quilt. This is a very important part of quiltmaking that will help stabilize your quilt center.

Straight Grain

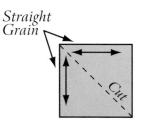

Straight Grain

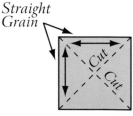

Corner Triangles

Side Triangles

Helpful Hints for Sewing with Flannel

Always prewash and machine dry flannel. This will prevent severe shrinkage after the quilt is made. Some flannels shrink more than others. For this reason, we have allowed approximately

1/4 yard extra for each fabric under the fabric requirements. Treat the more heavily napped side of solid flannels as the right side of the fabric.

Because flannel stretches more than other cotton calicos and because the nap makes them thicker, the quilt design should be simple. Let the fabric and color make the design statement.

Consider combining regular cotton calicos with flannels. The different textures complement each other nicely.

Use a 10 to 12 stitches per inch setting on your machine. A 1/4-inch seam allowance is also recommended for flannel piecing.

When sewing triangle-pieced squares together, take extra care not to stretch the diagonal seam. Trim off the points from the seam allowances to eliminate bulk.

Press gently to prevent stretching pieces out of shape.

Check block measurements as you progress. "Square up" the blocks as needed. Flannel will shift and it is easy to end up with blocks that are misshapen. If you trim and measure as you go, you are more likely to have accurate blocks. If you notice a piece of flannel is stretching more than the others, place it on the bottom when stitching on the machine.

The natural action of the feed dogs will help prevent it from stretching.

Before stitching pieces, strips, or borders together, pin often to prevent fabric from stretching and moving. When stitching longer pieces together, divide the pieces into quarters and pin. Divide into even smaller sections to get more control.

Use a lightweight batting to prevent the quilt from becoming too heavy.

Cutting Triangles from Squares

Cutting accurate triangles can be intimidating for beginners, but a clear acrylic ruler, rotary cutter, and cutting mat are all that are needed to make perfect triangles. The cutting instructions often direct you to cut strips, then squares, and then triangles.

Sewing Layered Strips Together

When you are instructed to layer strips, right sides together, and sew, you need to take some precautions. Gently lay one strip on top of another, carefully lining up the raw edges. Pressing the strips together will hold them together nicely, and a few pins here and there will also help. Be careful not to stretch the strips as you sew them together.

Choosing the Backing

The backing of any quilt is just as important to the overall design as the pieced patchwork top. Combine large-scale prints or piece coordinating fabrics together to create an interesting quilt back. Using large pieces of fabric (perhaps three different prints that are the same length as the quilt) or a large piece of fabric that is bordered by compatible prints, keeps the number of seams to a minimum, which speeds up the process. The new 108-inch wide fabric sold on the bolt eliminates the need for seaming entirely. Carefully selected fabrics for a well-constructed backing not only complement a finished quilt, but make it more useful as a reversible accent.

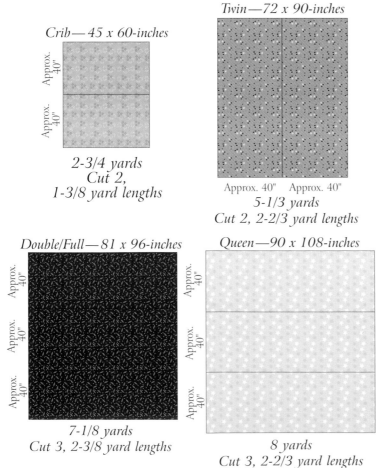

Crib—45 x 60-inches

Approx. 40"
Approx. 40"

2-3/4 yards
Cut 2,
1-3/8 yard lengths

Twin—72 x 90-inches

Approx. 40"   Approx. 40"
5-1/3 yards
Cut 2, 2-2/3 yard lengths

Double/Full—81 x 96-inches

Approx. 40"
Approx. 40"
Approx. 40"

7-1/8 yards
Cut 3, 2-3/8 yard lengths

Queen—90 x 108-inches

Approx. 40"
Approx. 40"
Approx. 40"

8 yards
Cut 3, 2-2/3 yard lengths

Finishing the Quilt

1. Remove the selvages from the backing fabric. Sew the long edges together and press. Trim the backing and batting so they are 4-inches to 6-inches larger than the quilt top.

2. Mark the quilt top for quilting. Layer the backing, batting, and quilt top. Baste the 3 layers together and quilt.

3. When quilting is complete, remove basting. Hand baste all 3 layers together a scant 1/4-inch from the edge. This hand basting keeps the layers from shifting and prevents puckers from forming when adding the binding. Trim excess batting and backing fabric even with the edge of the quilt top. Add the binding as shown below.

Binding and Diagonal Piecing

1. Diagonally piece the binding strips. Fold the strip in half lengthwise, wrong sides together, and press.

Diagonal Piecing

Stitch diagonally

Trim to 1/4-inch seam allowance

Press seam open

2. Unfold and trim one end at a 45-degree angle. Turn under the edge 3/8-inch and press. Refold the strip.

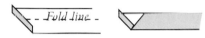

Double-layer Binding

3. With raw edges of the binding and quilt top even, stitch with a 3/8-inch seam allowance, starting 2-inches from the angled end.

4. Miter the binding at the corners. As you approach a corner of the quilt, stop sewing 3/8-inch from the corner of the quilt.

Quilt Top

5. Clip the threads and remove the quilt from under the presser foot. Flip the binding strip up and away from the quilt, then fold the binding down even with the raw edge of the quilt. Begin sewing at the upper edge. Miter all 4 corners in this manner.

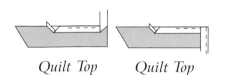

Quilt Top   *Quilt Top*

6. Trim the end of the binding so it can be tucked inside of the beginning binding about 1/2-inch. Finish stitching the seam.

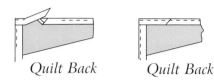

   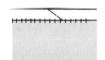

Quilt Back   *Quilt Back*

7. Turn the folded edge of the binding over the raw edges and to the back of the quilt so that the stitching line does not show. Hand sew the binding in place, folding in the mitered corners as you stitch.

Quilt Back   *Quilt Back*   *Quilt Back*

Quilt top Top layer of a quilt usually consisting of pieced blocks.

Quilting The small running stitches made through the layers of a quilt (quilt top, batting and backing) to form decorative patterns on the surface of the quilt and hold the layers together.

Quilting stencils Quilting patterns with open areas through which a design is transferred onto a quilt top. May be purchased or made from sturdy, reusable template plastic.

Rotary cutter Tool with a sharp, round blade attached to a handle that is used to cut fabric. The blade is available in different diameters.

Rotary cutting The process of cutting fabric into strips and pieces using a revolving blade rotary cutter, a thick, clear acrylic ruler, and a special cutting mat.

Running stitches A series of in-and-out stitches used in hand quilting.

Seam allowance The 1/4-inch margin of fabric between the stitched seam and the raw edge.

Selvage The lengthwise finished edge on each side of the fabric.

Slipstitch A hand stitch used for finishing such as sewing binding to a quilt where the thread is hidden by slipping the needle between a fold of fabric and tacking down with small stitches.

Squaring up or straightening fabric The process of trimming the raw edge of the fabric so it creates a 90-degree angle with the folded edge of the fabric. Squaring up is also a term used when trimming a quilt block.

Strip sets Two or more strips of fabric, cut and sewn together along the length of the strips.

Triangle-pieced square The square unit created when two 90-degree triangles are sewn together on the diagonal.

Unfinished size The measurement of a block before the 1/4-inch seam allowance is sewn or the quilt is quilted and bound.